Devin Durrant may be the most All-American of all the All-Americans I ever played with, and I played with a lot. He had great parenting and teaching, and was mature beyond his years. He knew who he was at such a young age. I can't think of anyone more qualified to write this book. I particularly like the "Be Your Own Coach" and "Make Your Own Luck" chapters. I can't wait to share some of his stories, quotes, and insights with my own children, and with some of the Boston Celtics players and coaches. This book is not only for parents raising children in sports, but for anyone who is playing, coaching, or teaching currently. Thank you, Devin, for sharing your experiences.

—DANNY AINGE

Boston Celtics Executive Director of Basketball Operations,
two-time NBA World Champion, and winner of the John Wooden Award

I loved to watch Devin play when we were both at BYU. Now, having read his book, I understand why he was able to accomplish what he and his teammates did back then. As I reflect back on my life, I see that whatever success I achieved came as a result of following the nine principles Devin clearly defines in his book. I look forward to putting the message of *Raising an All-American* into use with my own children. I wholeheartedly endorse this book for parents of young men and more importantly for the parents of many young women who desire to excel in sports and in life.

—SHARLENE WELLS HAWKES

Former Miss America, award-winning ESPN reporter,
and successful businesswoman

This book could be called "Blueprint for a Successful Life." Devin has outlined principles that are a roadway to success in all phases of life. He has done an excellent job of presenting the material in a way that can be easily understood and implemented by people of all ages. I particularly like the chapter, "Be Your Own Coach." Having coached many great players who were different in size, shape, potential, and talent, I found the ones who truly succeeded were those who took charge of their lives, became their "own coach," found out what they needed to do, were motivated and disciplined, and simply "did it." This book is a must for every home. Good job, Devin!

—LAVELL EDWARDS

Legendary BYU football coach, National Coach of the Year, and member of the College Football Hall of Fame

I loved this book. My favorite chapter was the mentally tough chapter. Devin calls it "rodeo tough." As I read this message, I thought of the successful athletes whom I have known. The most vivid memory I have of each one was his or her mental toughness. All nine parts of the All- American Puzzle are important. All are vital to success. But I personally love to watch those athletes who are mentally tough play the game. Devin, your book is awesome!

—TOM HOLMOE

Winner of Four Super Bowls with the San Francisco 49ers, three times as a player and once as a coach

Having coached numerous All-Americans, I know what it takes. It would be impossible for me to put into one book all I've taught these athletes. But Devin has done it in a manner that amazes me. His Nine Parts of the All-American Puzzle describe everything my athletes—male and female—need to do to reach their full potential. Devin teaches what it takes to transform a young man or woman into an All-American, not only in sports, but also in life.

—DAVE HOULE

The most successful high school coach in America with over 66 State Championships at Mountain View High School. Member of the National High School Hall of Fame

Having observed athletes over many years, I can attest to the importance of attitude and mental ability in athletics. Devin has succeeded in capturing in print the positive attributes needed for athletic success. He describes the mental toughness and determination it takes for the "All-American." This is a "must read" for the aspiring athlete, his or her parents, and those who support the aspiring athletes. Devin's common sense approach is presented in a manner that keeps interest. His light touches of humor with his blend of practical advice and positive principles present a well-rounded view on his approach to athletics and success in life. This book is a stirring recipe for success.

—RICK BOLUS

Publisher of the High Potential Basketball Recruiting Service

I really appreciate, as a parent and as a coach, Devin's insights on the importance of finding a balance in our lives. I love Devin's passion and commitment to the game and his model for the pursuit of excellence in athletics and in life. This book will be an inspiration to parents raising children in sports and a practical teaching tool for anyone involved in competitive athletics.

—STEVE CLEVELAND

Fresno State University head men's basketball coach

RAISING AN
ALL-AMERICAN

RAISING AN ALL-AMERICAN

HELPING YOUR CHILD EXCEL IN ATHLETICS (AND IN LIFE)

FEATURING THE 9 PARTS OF THE ALL-AMERICAN PUZZLE

DEVIN DURRANT
with his father, GEORGE DURRANT

WWW.RAISINGANALLAMERICAN.COM

spring creek
BOOK COMPANY
Provo, Utah

ISBN 13: 978-1-932898-41-5
ISBN 10: 1-932898-41-7
e. 1

Published by:
Spring Creek Book Company
P.O. Box 50355
Provo, Utah 84605-0355
www.springcreekbooks.com

Printed in the United States of America
10 9 8 7 6 5 4 3 2 1
Printed on acid-free paper

Library of Congress Cataloging-in-Publication Data
Durrant, Devin.
   Raising an all-american : helping your child succeed in athletics (and in life) /
Devin Durrant ; with George Durrant.
      p. cm.
   Summary: "Devin Durrant takes examples from his own All-American sports
career and the careers of other star athletes and uses them to illustrate how each
of the Nine Parts of the All-American Puzzle can be used by parents to help their
children to excel in any demanding pursuit--inside or outside the world of athletics"-
-Provided by publisher.
   Includes bibliographical references.
   ISBN-13: 978-1-932898-41-5 (pbk. : alk. paper)
   ISBN-10: 1-932898-41-7 (pbk. : alk. paper)
   1. Sports for children. 2. Parent and child. 3. Sports for children--Social aspects.
I. Durrant, George D. II. Title.

GV709.2.D89 2005
796'.083--dc22
                              2005011241

TABLE OF CONTENTS

PART 3: BE COACHABLE

PART 6: DARE MIGHTY THINGS

PART 7: LOVE THE GAME

PART 8: MAKE YOUR OWN LUCK

FOREWORD

BY STEPHEN R. COVEY

This is truly an amazing book. Parents will benefit enormously from its message and its lessons. The All-American idea is really a metaphor, a symbol, for raising an outstanding child—one who is confident, disciplined, and who both achieves and contributes significantly.

Every caring parent is committed to the character development of each child. Character is the essence of *primary greatness*. What the popular culture calls success—that is, reputation, prestige, position, wealth, etc.—is what we might call *secondary greatness*. This book focuses on both secondary *and* primary greatness. The authors give primary emphasis to the latter—that is, to character development and contribution.

Let me illustrate what I am trying to say here. Most people will admit that while growing up and going to school they did a lot of cramming. That is, in some way they figured out the system so that they could get the highest grades possible with the least possible effort. I, myself, was guilty of this. I thought I was clever and smart, never giving the slightest thought to whether "the hens would eventually come home to roost." I even remember bragging to my friends how I could get nearly straight A's with hardly ever cracking a book.

Most adults will admit that cramming was a common practice among their friends and associates. But you could ask these same adults if cramming would work on the farm—that is, forgetting to plant in the spring, flaking off all summer, then hitting it real hard in the fall to bring in the harvest. They laugh at this picture, knowing that it's ridiculous to think that you could cram on the farm and still bring in the harvest. Yet they did it all the time in school.

Why does cramming work in the school and not on the farm? The farm is a *natural* system, governed by *natural laws*, or what we could call *principles*. A school is a *social* system, manufactured through human effort and governed by *social laws*. That's why most people would acknowledge that you can get a degree without getting an education. Character development, including development of the mind, is also a natural system and is governed by natural laws or principles. It cannot be faked or pretended. It requires patience, persistence, and continuous and systematic effort, day in and day out.

Trust is the glue of life, and the building of high trust relationships is also a natural system, based upon natural laws or principles. Have you ever tried to talk yourself out of a problem you've behaved yourself into? How did it go? Have you ever seen a business try to PR itself out of a problem it has behaved itself into? How did that go?

What about sports at an All-American level? It, too, is obviously a natural system, governed by natural laws and principles. Any athlete knows that there isn't a way a person can cram themselves into excellence at the All-American level, no matter how talented or how outstanding their achievements at lower levels. You simply have to pay the price. There is no cramming.

This is why the All-American sports metaphor is so powerful, why it is directly correlated with what it takes to produce an "All-American" kid, whether in athletics, academics, social contribution, or in any area where real value is being added in a sustainable, superior way.

Parents need to raise their children in a *natural* system atmosphere, where no amount of pretense, cramming, short-cutting, or appearance will work.

Another reason why sports is such a powerful *natural* system analogy is because more and more, both boys and girls are getting caught up in fun sports activities. In most cases, they can find the sport which taps their interests and talents, where, if they are willing to pay the price, they can achieve success. As they gradually build into their character the habits, initiative, discipline, tough mindedness, physical fitness, and teamwork, they experience the irony that we need to cooperate in order to compete. In fact, I have come to believe that in many cases people can actually develop more character through high-level sports activity than academic studies, unless, of course, they bring the law of the farm into their academic studies. I didn't do this. Neither did most of my friends, and neither did most adults. But eventually the hens did come home to roost. While in graduate school, I ended up with ulcerative colitis from my feverish, almost frantic, effort to make up for four years of undergraduate cramming. When I could stand back and see what was happening to my life, I realized that what I thought was cleverness was nothing but foolish arrogance. So in my doctoral work, I organized and executed another undergraduate equivalent.

So what we're seeing here is that there are two realms—the *natural* and *social*—governed respectively by natural and social laws.

Another powerful theme, both explicit and implicit, which weaves itself through this entire book, is that young men and women, our children, have the power of choice. Next to life itself, the right to direct one's own life is the greatest gift we've been given. Most people, however, never fully exercise the power of choice in their lives. Most live out the "programs" they have been given—straitjackets to the natural gifts and potential hardwired into them at birth. Just as the most powerful of computers is entirely limited by the software through which it has to operate, so, too, are people—all with enormous potential—limited by the *social software* they are given. Unless they become deeply aware of their power to choose and determine to exercise this power in ways that are harmonious with natural laws or principles, they will remain undeveloped. Instead of living, they will be lived—selling one's birthright for a mess of social potage.

I once had a powerful experience that taught me this principle while on a sabbatical in Hawaii. I had been studying the success literature of our country going back to its founding, and realized that little by little we had moved away from the character ethic based on principles into a personality ethic that focused more on techniques, image, appearance, and technologies. In other words, we moved from primary to secondary greatness. I had just completed this literature review and was in a very reflective state of mind, thinking about its implications. While in this state, I was wandering through the stacks at the library in Hawaii one day, and pulled down a book that had three sentences which absolutely staggered me. They changed my life and gave me a foundation for my own work. These three sentences are these:

Between stimulus and response is a space.

In that space lies our freedom and power to choose
our response.

In those choices lie our growth and our happiness.

In other words, between all things that have ever happened to us or are now happening to us, and our response to those things, there lies a space in which our freedom to choose our response resides. This applies even to our biological inheritance, between our genetic tendencies and our response to them. Many people have predispositions toward certain diseases, such as diabetes or cancer. But if they will exercise this self-awareness and their power of freedom and act on the basis of natural laws or principles regarding proper health prevention practices and medical assistance, they will, in many cases, not contract the very disease to which they had the genetic predisposition, and if they do they can usually "nip it in the bud" through early detection.

This is an extremely powerful idea, because it means that we may not be free *from* things that have happened to us, but we are free *to* accomplish what we set our hearts upon. In other words, we are influenced by our circumstances, our past social conditioning, upbringing, and genetic inheritance, but we are *not determined* by them. The difference between being influenced by and determined by is 180 degrees. Taking responsibility makes each person a creative force of his or her own life, and if young children grow up with such teaching and this kind of family encouragement and nurturance, they will literally be capable of applying the nine powerful puzzle parts or principles discussed in this book. They will also be able to be an observer of their own participation in athletics or any other significant activity. Because of that self-aware observation, they can become their own coach, as beautifully taught herein. They can also learn to benefit from the coaches assigned to them and can run with their strengths and compensate for their weaknesses through self-coaching, self-management and complementary role-playing so their strengths are made productive and their weaknesses become essentially irrelevant.

Animals can't do this, no matter how intelligent they may be. They cannot reinvent themselves. They simply lack self-awareness. They are a product of their biological inheritance and their conditioning/training. This book is filled with the spirit of what I'm talking about here and is a magnificent message for children to grow up with. They do not give their power away. They cease to become victims of circumstances. Victims give their futures away, literally. Today and tomorrow are held hostage by yesterday. People who are self-aware exercise the initiative to act on the nine principles of this book and can *create* their own futures. Their very example will inspire others, which is the essence of leadership—to communicate to other people their worth and potential so clearly they come to see it in themselves. This is what parents can do for their own children.

Two other extremely powerful and practical themes are communicated in this book which I believe most parents will want their children to deeply buy into. First, fortune favors the bold. In other words, when people take initiative and are appropriately aggressive, not only in sports, but in their life, great things can happen. They become the creative force of their own life and come to understand that the key to predicting one's future is to create it.

The second theme is how balanced this material is in terms of the four dimensions of life—the physical/economic, the social/relationship, the mental, and the spiritual. Parents, teachers and youth leaders, as well as athletically inclined young people, will sense the importance of an integration of these four dimensions and the importance of balance in life, in giving security, wisdom, guidance and power, particularly when these dimensions are based upon principles, or natural laws.

A brief final word about the author, Devin Durrant, and his helping co-author father, George Durrant. These are people filled with integrity; what they write about is what they live.

Even though Devin was given the designation of All-American because of his basketball accomplishments, all of George and Marilyn's kids are All-American in the primary greatness sense. George has authored many outstanding books and has been a remarkable teacher of thousands of people.

Both Devin and George have the human touch, and that touch can be felt throughout this entire book. Readers can feel assured that they are dealing with authentic, real people. They have been around the block many times and write with deep conviction, wisdom, and moral authority. I am so proud to comment on this outstanding work. I commend to you, dear reader, a serious study of these natural laws, these principles of life.

You know, this is fundamentally a book on excellent parenting.

Stephen R. Covey
April 2005

PREFACE

MY FAMILY

My name is Devin Durrant. I love sports. I am a 44-year-old father of four daughters and two sons. My wife and I have been married for 22 years. She and I decided early on in our marriage that we wanted our children to participate in sports as they grew up. We felt by having our children participate in sports, they would learn valuable lessons that would serve them well throughout their entire lives. Sports can be an excellent teacher of some of life's most important lessons. And, unless you are raising your kids on a farm, participation in athletics might be the best chance for your children to learn some of these valuable life lessons.

This book is about parents helping children to succeed athletically and learning lessons through athletic participation that will help them find success in life. Let me start by telling you about my family and our affection for sports. My dad loved sports. From my earliest memory, my dad steered my four brothers, three sisters, and me in the direction of sports. As a young boy, I remember my dad telling me stories about my Uncle Kent who was a standout high school basketball player in the late 1940s.

Dad told me that my Uncle Kent was the first high school player in the state of Utah to dunk a basketball during a game.

Dad also told us fictional stories of great athletes who did amazing things on the baseball diamond, on the basketball court, or on the football field. My favorite fictional character was Rip Snorgan. He was the finest athlete to ever play for Snodgrass High School. His best friend was a girl by the name of Fanny Foofoo. Fanny was also a stellar athlete. My Dad's stories about the amazing accomplishments of Rip and Fanny made me want to be a great athlete.

As time passed and I grew older, I had the pleasure of witnessing some incredible feats on the field of competition. Some of the feats were more incredible than the fictional ones that were related to me by my father. From the great athletes I watched during my growing up years, I started to gain an understanding of what it might require to become the athlete that I wanted to be. Now as I reflect back on my life, I feel that I have developed a formula for success in sports, and more importantly, a formula for success in life. That is what I want to offer you on the pages of this book.

Before I go any further, I want to introduce you to each of my children. Emily is my oldest daughter. She is now a junior in college. During her junior high and high school years she played competitive basketball. She experimented with track and volleyball, but basketball was her joy. She loved the game and her teams were very successful. Her biggest battle as an athlete was with pain. She struggled with shin splints throughout her career but somehow found a way to play with pain and enjoy the fruits of her hard work as an athlete. Last night, she came home from the gym with a smile on her face. She still enjoys a good game of basketball.

Laura is my second oldest daughter. She played some basketball in junior high but then decided she did not want to follow in her older sister's footsteps. She decided to compete in volleyball. She played for her school team from the ninth grade through the eleventh grade. She enjoyed a lot of success with her volleyball teammates during those three years. However, during her senior year, she decided not to play volleyball. She realized she would be playing behind one of her closest friends who was an excellent athlete so she decided to switch sports. She joined the cross-country and track teams. I hated to see her leave volleyball because I felt that she was a terrific player but I understood her feelings of wanting to play rather than sit the bench because I sure hated to spend any time on the bench. I was glad she decided to run with her high school team. I am a runner at heart and I loved watching her run. She has a magnificent running stride. She was an Academic All-State cross-country runner. She is now a freshman in college and occasionally she and I will run together.

Heather is my third daughter. She also chose to play competitive volleyball. She competed in that sport for four years beginning in the seventh grade. I loved to watch her compete as a setter because she had such soft hands and a will to win. I'll never forget watching her sob after her team lost to a cross-town rival. She is a very mellow person on the outside with a strong will to win on the inside. She stopped playing volleyball after her sophomore year because she didn't like the stress and tension that her coach created at practice and games. I wish she would have continued on with volleyball because I think that her coach, because of her tough style, could have helped her become an excellent volleyball player. However, Heather had other plans and I supported her. This past year, she has been playing a lot of tennis. She competed in doubles for her high school with one of her best friends as her partner, but her season was cut short due to a wrist injury. I believe she will try again to compete in tennis during her senior year. She likes tennis because she feels that it is a sport she can enjoy for a lifetime.

Ryan is my 13-year-old son. He just completed his first year of tackle football. He is learning to be a more physical athlete, which is kind of difficult for the skinny 100 pounder that he is. He has also played both Little League baseball and basketball. Last night he got a call from a coach informing him that he had made the seventh grade basketball "A" team. He was thrilled as he reported the phone call to my wife and me.

Joseph is my second son. He is nine years old. He loves flag football and looks forward to the day when his mother allows him to play tackle football. He has also played Little League baseball and basketball. I love to watch Joseph compete because he gives everything he has to help his team win.

Deanna is my baby. She is seven years old. She was recently the winner of her division in a 3k race in our city. She may be my best athlete. She is currently enjoying her first year of organized soccer. She wants to do anything that her older brothers get to do. She is a regular participant at our house in basketball shooting games, baseball hitting games, and touch football games.

My wife, Julie, also loves sports. She was a cheerleader and a songleader in high school. In college she was the quarterback for her intramural football team. She currently serves as a rebounder for our two sons. She has spent a large chunk of her life watching sporting events live and on television. She has also logged many miles in her van shuttling our children to and from practices.

As you can see, sports play a major role in the Durrant family. Yes, there is more to our lives than just sports. My kids have all learned to play the piano. They all do well in school. The boys are involved in scouting. And we are all active in our church. But there should be no doubt about the fact that the Durrant family loves sports.

I believe that sports can bless any family in a variety of ways.

A prime example of that can be found in the Pat Williams family. Pat is the senior vice-president of the NBA's Orlando Magic. He has been involved in professional sports as a participant and as a front office executive. He relates the following about his amazing family:

> We have nineteen children, and they all played sports. Fourteen of them are adopted, and the minute they got off the airplane from South Korea, the Philippines, Romania, or Brazil, I got a glove in their hand or got them into the swimming pool, or put soccer shoes on them, and got them involved immediately. Through all those youth sports, and through all the Little League periods, and on into high school, I think it was one of the most important things I did for them. If nothing else, it let them experience the magic of teamwork, getting along with other people. The self-discipline that it takes, the hard work that's involved, the respect of coaches, all that is so important. I fully believe that the life lessons learned by these children—who had come off the streets from Third World countries—will never leave them. That's why I encourage parents to expose their children to sports, even if they aren't great athletes. [1]

I share Pat's feelings and encourage you to involve your children in sports, whether they become All-Americans or learn to play for the simple enjoyment of friendly competition. Regardless of the success your child might attain in the world of sports, the more important goal is to help your child excel in life. Participation in sports can help you achieve that greater goal.

The lessons taught in this book can be learned to a certain degree in other arenas—on the farm, in the marching band, and so on. But it is tough to find an arena better than sports wherein a young person can learn about overcoming trials, dealing with failure, handling success, understanding human relations, playing a role, developing a strong work ethic, responding to criticism, dealing with stress, being a leader, being a follower, staying true to your values, or building character. The list of lessons could go on. It is my hope that, over the years, sports will bless the lives of you and your children as they have mine.

REACH FOR THE TOP

The purpose of this book is to teach you how to raise an All-American—a child who is capable of excelling athletically and in life. The reality is that only a few of you will be able to raise an athlete who is named to an All-American team. Don't be discouraged. Your child will learn and grow so much in the pursuit of athletic excellence that the effort will be well worth it. The rewards will be seen in all areas of your child's life.

THE PRINCIPLES APPLY TO ALL PURSUITS OF EXCELLENCE

In this book, I use examples from a variety of sports. I use experiences from both male and female athletes to make my points. I share many of my own experiences as a father of six and as an athlete to illustrate how the various parts of the All-American Puzzle can come together. Another name for the All-American Puzzle could be the Excellence Puzzle. For me, All-American and excellence are synonymous. While my examples and stories may not apply to your child's particular pursuit of excellence, I believe that the nine principles I teach in this book apply not only to all sports but to any person's climb to the top inside or outside the world of sports.

THE TEAM COMES FIRST

An easy criticism to make of this book is that I focus on individual achievement. That can be viewed as a big negative in team sports. However, the underlying spirit of my message is that if your child becomes the best he or she can possibly be, he or she will naturally be helping the team become better. Also, keep in mind that it is rare for an All-American to play on a losing team. The team comes first, the individual second. That will always be true in team sports.

YOU DECIDE WHAT YOU WANT YOUR CHILD TO READ

As you read the following chapters, have a marker in hand to highlight what you think would be beneficial for your child to read. Encourage your child to read the portions of the book that you have highlighted. Then, together, discuss the highlighted sections. From these discussions, you will be able to formulate ideas as to how to best help your child as he or she strives for excellence.

SMOOTH COMMUNICATION

Let me say a few things at the outset that will help us communicate throughout the book. This book is addressed to fathers and mothers or any other significant adult who wants to help a young person succeed.

In order to eliminate the frequent use of phrases like "your son and daughter" and "he or she" and "mother and father," I address myself to fathers and sons most of the time. I ask you to translate any masculine word or phrase to the relationship you are in, whether it is father-daughter, mother-daughter, mother-son, and so on. The term "father" can also be replaced by the term "mother" or "parents."

It is not my intent to leave mothers or girls out of the All-American process. I know how much my mother meant to my development. I can also see what a vital role my wife is playing in raising my sons and daughters so that they can be successful on the court and off. I simply want to provide a smooth reading highway for you to travel on throughout this book.

I should also mention at this point that I have never been

more excited at basketball games than I was during my daughter Emily's high school years. I know firsthand that having a daughter out on the court is an equal source of satisfaction and joy to having a son out there. I believe that athletics does as much for women as it does for men. However, in writing this book I found it extremely difficult to address both males and females at the same time in every instance. For that reason, I address the male parent even though my message is for both fathers and mothers.

REPETITION

In this book I discuss nine principles of excellence. Because these principles overlap each other to a certain degree, I will occasionally, of necessity and on purpose, make similar points more than once.

SLEEPLESS NIGHTS

Every now and then I have a very difficult time getting to sleep. It usually means that I am excited about something and I can't get my mind to slow down and my body to relax. Roughly 20 years ago, I read the book *Creating Wealth* by Robert Allen. I distinctly remember how I felt after I read that book. It made it very difficult for me to sleep for several nights because it got me so excited about real estate investment. That book was the beginning of my present career—a career that has brought me a satisfaction in many ways similar to the satisfaction I felt as an athlete.

I hope as you read this book, you have some sleepless nights as you think of ways you can help your child achieve success. I hope you can see a vision of your child's future accomplishments and I hope that vision becomes reality in future years.

MY CO-AUTHOR

My co-author is my father. The main reason I asked him to help me with this book was because he has done what the title of the book suggests—he raised an All-American. He has been the perfect father for me. He, in his own magical way, helped me find and place every piece in my All-American Puzzle. For that I will always be in his debt. But he did more than just raise one All-American. He and my mother raised eight children who all went on to excellence in their chosen fields. Thank you, Mom and Dad!

WHAT HAPPENED TO ME AFTER COLLEGE?

While I was indeed an All-American at the college level, I wasn't as successful at the professional level. I played for a year with the Indiana Pacers and briefly for the Phoenix Suns. I then went to Europe and played for two seasons in Spain and for part of a third season in France. So while I was able to get a paycheck as a professional basketball player for about five years after college, I would be considered a bust as a professional athlete.

The thoughts I share with you in this book come from times of great accomplishment as well as moments of disappointing failure. May your successes always far outweigh your failures. However, I have learned in my life, as you will see in this book, that while success is much more enjoyable, valuable lessons can be learned from failure.

INTRODUCTION

Michael Jordan, Charles Barkley, Hakeem Olajuwon, Patrick Ewing, and Devin Durrant. Which name doesn't belong? The answer is obvious. It is my name, Devin Durrant. However, 21 years ago, in 1984, my name did belong in that group. That is when I, along with the others mentioned above, was named by the national media as a college All-American in the sport of basketball.

I made All-American when I logically should not have. I was a skinny, six-foot seven-inch white kid with only average speed from the state of Utah. How did I do it? I did it by interlocking all the pieces of what I call, The All-American Puzzle. Let me explain.

LIKE ASSEMBLING A PICTURE PUZZLE

Imagine you are about to put together a 500-piece picture puzzle. You know the process. First, you separate the pieces into logical groups. If you were going to put together a puzzle that depicted a mountain scene, you might group the pieces as follows: In one group, you would place all the border pieces. Next, you would gather all the blue sky pieces. You would also create a pile for all the mountain pieces. Then you would have a pile for all the pieces that made up the mountain stream. You get the idea. Individual pieces, grouped together, are then interlocked to make up the various parts of the puzzle. All the parts, when connected, make up the puzzle. A puzzle is not complete unless every piece is placed in its correct location. To raise an All-American, you, as a parent, will need to do your part to help your son or daughter locate and place each piece where it belongs in his or her All-American Puzzle.

THE ALL-AMERICAN PUZZLE IS MADE UP OF NINE PARTS

In a careful analysis of my sports career and the careers of other successful athletes, I have found that in order to become an All-American there are nine basic principles or parts an athlete has to put together in order to complete the All-American Puzzle. These nine parts are:

1. The Dream
2. Be Your Own Coach
3. Be Coachable
4. Work, Work, Work
5. Rodeo Tough
6. Dare Mighty Things
7. Love The Game
8. Make Your Own Luck
9. Gifts From God

There are no shortcuts in assembling a picture puzzle. The same is true in becoming an All-American. In both cases the assembler has to put the end product together one piece at a time. The interlocked pieces make up the various parts, and the parts make up the puzzle. Finally, after tremendous effort, all the parts come together. The dream becomes a reality.

All the pieces of the first eight parts of the All-American Puzzle can be put together by your child if he or she desires it. It is up to your child. However, the pieces of the last part of the puzzle are gifts from above. Neither you nor your child has any say in this part of the puzzle. I'll say more about that in Part Nine.

DEVIN DURRANT'S
ALL-AMERICAN PUZZLE

PART 1
THE DREAM

MY DREAM

As a small boy, I loved to hear my Dad tell stories, true and fictional, of great athletic achievement. I dreamed of becoming a great athlete. I enjoyed playing sports from the time I can remember playing with and against my older brother. I always wanted to win. I learned early that winning was fun and playing well was thrilling. When I reached the third grade I started to dream of playing high school sports and maybe someday being on television.

During my early years, my dream of becoming a great athlete was based on fun and games. Then, in the eighth grade, my dream ran smack into reality.

COACH RICK BOLUS

I can't remember when I first heard the name Rick Bolus. It must have been during my seventh grade year. I do remember the stories that were going around about him. Rick Bolus was the coach of the ninth grade team at Seneca High School in Louisville, Kentucky. At the time, my older brother Matt was in the tenth grade. From him and his friends I heard stories

about the toughness of Coach Rick Bolus. One story was that
Coach Bolus made his team run so hard a guy collapsed and
had to crawl to the locker room at the end of practice. Another
story was told of a time when Coach Bolus grabbed one of his
players' jerseys, got in his face, yelled at him, and then spit on
his jersey. I don't know if any of the stories I heard were true.
I do know that I was very scared of Coach Bolus. He looked
mean. He had dark hair, a dark complexion, piercing eyes, a
black mustache, and crooked teeth. Maybe his teeth weren't
really crooked. How would I know? I never saw him smile.

Seneca Junior High School (seventh and eighth grades)
was housed in a separate wing connected to Seneca Senior
High School (ninth through twelfth grades). Occasionally,
as a seventh grader, I had to go into the high school area for
one reason or another. Sometimes the shortest path to where
I needed to go passed by Mr. Bolus' class. When that was the
case I would take a different, longer route.

During my seventh grade year I played on the junior high
team along with other seventh and eighth graders. I don't
remember much from that season other than the embarrassment
I felt from my purple high-top shoes. My mother bought them
for me because they were on sale. It was either wear purple or
wear my old worn-out shoes. I went with purple. We didn't
have much money back then and my Mom didn't seem to care
about the importance of wearing the right shoe color. After a
while, my teammates stopped teasing me.

My seventh grade year soon ended. During the summer
between my seventh and eighth grade years I played a lot of
basketball. I loved playing on the hoop at the side of our house.
Alex Montgomery, my best friend, was with me a lot of the
time. We loved to play basketball together.

During that summer, an adult friend of our family, Steve
White, invited my older brother, Matt, and me to play in a
pickup game at our church. For some reason Rick Bolus was

there. After we played, Steve told my brother and me that Rick was a friend of his. I didn't think someone that mean had any friends. Steve mentioned that Rick might be my coach that fall, and he encouraged me to try out for the ninth grade team as an eighth grader. I had never considered that option before. I was simply planning on playing with the seventh and eighth grade team as I had done the year before. This new thought of trying out for the ninth grade team as an eighth grader and playing for Coach Bolus gave me nightmares. I loved basketball. Why ruin it by playing with guys who were older and much better than I was and by playing for a madman who terrified me?

Time passed and school started. I was now 13 years old and in the eighth grade. I continued to take the long route to avoid Mr. Bolus' classroom. Somehow I found out about the upcoming tryouts for the ninth grade team. They were going to be held a couple of weeks before the seventh and eighth grade team tryouts.

Along with all the horror stories I had heard about Coach Bolus, I was told that he had been a great college basketball player a few years earlier. He had been the third-leading scorer in the country, averaging 33 points a game during his freshman year at the Virginia Military Institute. He then went on to finish his college basketball years at Boston College. *He must know the game*, I thought to myself. *I could learn a lot from him.* Maybe the killer stories I had heard weren't as bad as they sounded. Over time I talked myself into trying out for his team. I figured that he would cut me and then I would be ready to return to my friends on the seventh and eighth grade team.

Tryouts began and I quickly realized that I had made a big mistake. Coach Bolus taught us, yelled at us, and then we ran. He then taught us some more, yelled at us some more, and then we ran some more. Teach, yell, run was a daily pattern. After a few days, I wanted to quit. It would have been so much easier with the guys my own age. The coach of the younger team was a former baseball player and he wasn't crazy like Coach Bolus. But I couldn't quit. I figured if I quit, Coach Bolus would come looking for me. I was afraid of what might happen when he found me. So I continued to show up for practice. My last hope was that Coach Bolus would cut me and end my misery. The final cuts came and I made the team as the only eighth grader on the ninth grade team. One part of me was thrilled with the achievement while the other part of me dreaded the fact I would be under the direction of Rick Bolus for the next five months.

Coach Bolus wasted no time preparing us for the upcoming season. He demanded our undivided attention, absolute respect, and our very best effort every time we stepped on the floor. He came from a military background and from him I got a taste of what boot camp must be like. When we spoke to Coach Bolus, we started with sir and ended with sir. For example, if you wanted a drink of water, you would say, "Sir, may I get a drink of water, sir?" He had an effective way of eliminating mistakes on the floor. If you made a bad pass, he would ask you what you did wrong. You would then say, "Sir, I made a bad pass, sir." He would then say, "I can't hear you." You would then yell as loud as you could, "Sir, I made a bad pass, sir." This would continue until Coach Bolus was satisfied that you would not make another bad pass any time soon. If he wanted to get a point across to the whole team, he would say, "Get on the line." That was the phrase he used to let us know that we had made a mistake and that we were going to run ladders until he felt that he had made his point. Under Coach Bolus we referred to "ladders" as "suicides." It seemed like a more fitting term at the time. If you don't know what running a "ladder" or a "suicide" means, consider yourself fortunate. They are painful.

Soon the games started. As a team we were very successful. We didn't lose often because we were well prepared and because we all feared the punishment we would receive if we lost. I remember after one loss, Coach Bolus taught us the meaning of an Indian Run. He started us running around the gym in single file. He then told the last guy to sprint to the front of the line. When he arrived at the front of the line, the last guy in line then had to sprint to the front of the line.

If he felt that anyone was not sprinting when it was his turn he would say, "Get on the line." We would then stop the Indian Run and run "suicides" for a while. Coach Bolus would then give us another "opportunity" to try and get the Indian Run right. Occasionally he would give us a break from running to teach us what we had done in the previous game that caused us to lose. We would then run some more so that we would remember to not make the same mistakes again.

Coach Bolus made us tough physically and mentally. He simulated high-pressure situations in practice that forced us to concentrate on the tasks at hand. He prepared us to play physical basketball. He had a drill we did as a team that made each of us tougher physically. He had one team member stand in a circle with a basketball. The other team members surrounded him and locked arms. Then the one in the middle was told to fight his way out while holding the basketball. If he got out of the circle, all the members of the circle were told to "get on the line." If the man in the middle didn't get out, he was given the chance to "get on the line."

I will never forget the day Coach Bolus stopped practice and put himself into the scrimmage we were having. He then said that he was going to guard me. We started to play and he pushed me, shoved me, backed into me, and fouled me. I continued to try to run the offense and play defense as I had been instructed. Finally, after dishing out a good pounding on me, Coach Bolus stopped practice and looked at me. "Are you ever going to fight back," he asked. I didn't know what to say. He then told me that I needed to get tougher and to not let others push me around so much.

We started the scrimmage again. He continued to pound on me, but now I started to pound back. I pushed him when he pushed me. I even banged into him before he could do the same to me. Finally, he stopped the scrimmage, looked at me, and said, "That's better." He then took himself out of the scrimmage.

Coach Bolus taught me a valuable lesson. He knew I was a soft kid, but he saw something special in me. He saw the potential for excellence but he knew for me to succeed, I would have to be a lot tougher than I was at that time. He put me on the right road that day.

As the season progressed, I felt like I was improving a lot as a player. However, I still feared Coach Bolus more than any other person alive. He stretched me and my teammates beyond any and all limits we might have placed on ourselves. None of us liked Coach Bolus. We hated the man. He made our lives miserable. We did enjoy winning, however, and we did that a lot.

At about the midpoint of the season, the seventh and eighth grade coach approached me and asked if Coach Bolus would allow me to practice a few times with his team in preparation for some upcoming games. Up to that point in the season, I had only practiced with the ninth grade team but I had played in some games with the younger team when there was no conflict with a ninth grade game or practice. I loved the idea of practicing with the guys my own age.

I remember asking Coach Bolus if he would mind if I practiced a few times with the younger team so that I could blend a little better with them during games. He looked at me with those dark eyes and asked, "What would you like to do?" I knew what I wanted to do but I was afraid to tell Coach Bolus. I finally mumbled I thought it might be helpful if I could practice a bit with the younger team. He stared at me and said, "I never want to see you again." Then he turned around and left.

I was stunned. I had let Coach Bolus down. I didn't quite

know what to do. In my 13-year-old mind I decided I'd better forget about practicing with the younger guys. Coach Bolus was trying to teach me that the way to improve was by taking the difficult path, the challenging path. The next day I showed up at Coach Bolus' practice. Nothing was said, but I think he was glad to see me. The thought of practicing with the seventh and eighth grade team was eliminated from my mind.

Finally, the season I thought would never end, ended. I had never worked as hard as I worked during that season. Coach Bolus never let up the whole time he coached us. Our season was very successful.

After the last game I turned in my uniform and left the gym. While I was sad that the season had ended, I felt an exhilarating freedom at the same time. No more Coach Bolus! No more aching legs and burning lungs! If that was the kind of effort it took to be a successful basketball player then I wasn't interested. I would just play for fun.

For the next couple of weeks I did nothing physical. I ate large bowls of ice cream and watched a lot of television. Life was good. Then one day I started to feel bored. I needed something to do. I picked up my basketball and went out on my court. I started to shoot baskets and to think. I loved basketball. I wanted to be good. I dreamed of being great. I felt like now I had an idea of what it was going to take to excel. I had hated Rick Bolus. I had hated playing for him. But I was starting to see how much he had done for me. He had helped me form a foundation under my dream.

SUPPORTING YOUR CHILD'S DREAM

Hopefully there will be a Rick Bolus in your child's athletic life. If not just one tough coach, then a composite of coaches who will be "Rick Bolus Tough." Ideally, these coaches will be tough enough to test your young athlete to the core. Tough enough they could extinguish his dream if it were not for your love and support of him. I didn't tell my parents much about Rick Bolus. But they knew he was there. They knew it was hard for me. They loved me and built me up in ways only parents can.

Dreams are pretty delicate. It doesn't take much discouragement or doubt to squash a dream. A dream is like the first little flame that could be the beginning of a bonfire. It can be blown out by a single breath. You as a parent need to be there to shelter the young flame and to help your child find the fuel to build the flame into a mighty fire.

Rick Bolus had built a foundation under my dream that I could now build on. He taught me about respect, discipline, hard work, toughness, and character. He taught me responsibility. What he taught me wasn't much fun at the time but I would not have become an All-American without Coach Bolus in my life. Through it all, my parents were there for me, and if they had not been, my dream might have slowly faded away.

My eighth grade year was the last season Coach Bolus acted as the ninth grade coach. He moved on to other coaching positions and now runs the High Potential Basketball Recruiting Service, which is widely recognized as the best scouting and recruiting service in the country. He is also one of the co-directors of the highly successful "Blue Chip" basketball camp held every summer in Georgetown, Kentucky.

My story of the season I spent with Rick Bolus is a simple story, but for me that season made all the difference. There were 11 others who were on that team with me. Two of us went on to play college ball. The others ended their basketball careers at high school graduation. But all of us, particularly me, were better prepared to deal with life because we had had the honor of playing under the direction of a great coach.

I went on and played my ninth grade year of basketball in Kentucky without Coach Bolus. My new team, under the

direction of a new coach, had a successful season together—
we won the Jefferson County championship. That was a great
feeling of accomplishment.

THE REST OF THE STORY

After my ninth grade year, my family moved from Kentucky
to Utah. Three years later, at the conclusion of my senior
basketball season at Provo High School, one of my dreams
came true. I was invited to return to Louisville, Kentucky, as
a McDonald's All-American to compete in the Derby Festival
Basketball Classic, which matched the Kentucky-Indiana All-
Stars against the United States All-Stars. It was a great day
for me. I was the winner of the one-on-one competition held
among all the players from both teams that morning. That night
we beat the Kentucky-Indiana All-Stars and I was named the
Most Valuable Player of the game. My parents were there to
cheer me on.

One of the highlights of the weekend for me was seeing
Coach Rick Bolus. He smiled when he saw me. That was the
first time I think I had ever seen him smile. I was so pleased to
think Coach Bolus was happy with my progress.

A few years later, Coach Bolus and my old friend, Steve
White, drove up to Indianapolis from Louisville to see me play
in the NBA as a rookie for the Indiana Pacers. I think it must
have been satisfying for Coach Bolus to see how far I had come
since we first met many years earlier, knowing he was the man
that laid the foundation for me to build on.

HELP YOUR CHILD SEE THE DREAM

Good coaches are certainly an important part of helping an
athlete turn a dream into a reality. However, one of the joys of
parenthood is the opportunity of helping young children see in
their minds their first images of their life's dreams.

Paul O'Neill of New York Yankee fame had a father who

helped him see a dream of what he could become. His father
told him that the way he held his bat reminded him of baseball
great Ted Williams. Paul O'Neill relates the following about
how his father helped him see a vision of his future:

> Another day not long after that, [my father] followed
> up his earlier remark [about Ted Williams] by walking
> up to me and putting his hand on my shoulder, peering
> down into my eyes, and saying, "You're going to be a
> major-leaguer one day, Paul."
>
> For all I knew, this was a rite of passage, a comment
> he'd made to each one of my brothers—each of whom had
> tremendous baseball talent and professional potential.
> After all, I was only six. Didn't all fathers say that to their
> sons? But there was something in Dad's eyes, a magical
> gleam, that made me feel . . . who knew, maybe he was
> right? Maybe that was going to be my future?
>
> For a few weeks, I put it out of my mind, realizing I
> had a lot more growing up to do before I set my sights on
> any professional career. But when, that very summer, Dad
> announced that he and I were going to drive to Cincinnati
> so I could see my first Major League game—the Reds
> against the Pittsburgh Pirates—I couldn't get the dream
> out of my head. [1]

Give your child the gift Paul O'Neill's father gave him—
a dream of future success.

DEVIN DURRANT'S
ALL-AMERICAN PUZZLE

PART 2
BE YOUR OWN COACH

THE MOST IMPORTANT PART OF THE PUZZLE

If you asked me which part of the All-American Puzzle is the most important, I would answer that this part—the part dealing with being your own coach—is the most important. Your child can miss some other parts and still do well athletically. However, if he does not become his own coach he will never reach his full potential. Other coaches can get an athlete started up the mountain, but to reach the summit of greatness he must, on his own, go far beyond where a coach can lead him. He must ascend to a height where only his own will and work can take him. To become an All-American, an athlete must learn to be his own coach.

Coach Bolus gave my basketball dreams a great boost when I was in the eighth grade. But for me, things really took off a week or so after the season was over. It was then that I knew that he was no longer there to force me to do anything or to drive me to keep playing even when I was tired. It was that day—not because I had to but because I wanted to—that I set out on the road to becoming a player. On that day I put the ice cream spoon down, turned off the television, picked up a basketball, and went out into the heat and the humidity of a Kentucky afternoon and started to play. That was the day I became an All-American.

THE HEART OF THE ALL-AMERICAN DREAM

In the summer basketball camps I conducted over a nine-year period after I graduated from college, I did many things I thought were important for the young people who attended. I learned the name of each camper. I gave each of them individual attention. I encouraged them. I hired coaches with excellent teaching skills to help with the camp. Together we taught the campers a variety of skill improvement drills. I gave them a booklet I had compiled that included drills that they could do after the camp and a few motivational stories.

I loved those young kids who shared a dream of greatness. But the gift I tried to give them that was of most value was the understanding that in order to get better and better as a player, they had to be their own coach. To help them remember the importance of being their own coach, I would tell them the following story—Bossing Johnson. I also included a copy of this story in their camp booklet. To me this story conveys a very powerful message.

At least once a year, Dr. Spencer J. McCallie, a great southern educator, told the story about a little red-haired freckled-faced boy named Johnson who got a job at a large plant as an errand boy in the shipping department. Every day it was "Johnson, do this"..."Johnson, do that"..."Johnson, go here and...Johnson go there"..."Johnson, bring this to me"..."Johnson take that to him." Everyone in the plant bossed him. After several weeks of this, his temper started to churn and he went to his boss and told him that He Had Had It! The boss could take his job, and go jump in a lake.

The boss, being rather amused at the kid's spunk, said to Johnson, "How would you like to have someone to boss?" Johnson's eyes flashed, and a little cynical smile crept across that freckled face as he said, "More than anything on earth. Where is he? I'll kill him." The boss said, "His name is Johnson and he is in your department." Johnson looked rather amazed and said, "I am the only Johnson in the shipping department." The boss smiled and said, "I know. See what you can do with him."

Johnson went home that night and couldn't get out of his mind what the boss had said. The more he thought of it, the more he liked the idea. At least he could take his wrath out on someone. The next morning the alarm clock rang, and Johnson said, "Aw, we got another 20 or 30 minutes to soak here in the bed." . . . "Not on your life," he said, and jerked Johnson out of the bed and into the bathroom. "Wash between your ears, comb your hair, and put on a clean shirt. Lately you've looked like a bum. Then go to the plant at least 30 minutes early."

When the other employees arrived, the shipping department was swept clean, the boxes and corks neatly stacked in place on the tables, and Johnson was working his little head off at his post. Days, weeks, and months passed. He was so busy bossing Johnson, he never really remembered his first raise or his first promotion . . . raise followed raise and promotion followed promotion.

In time, Johnson sat at the head of that great corporation. He wasn't there by accident or because his family owned controlling stock. No, he was there because years earlier a little red-haired, freckled-faced boy booted him rung by rung from the bottom to the top of the ladder.

This story so easily translates into sports. As long as your child's coach is someone else, he will go as far as the coach can take him. But once your young athlete decides to be his own boss, up the ladder he will go, all the way to the top, all the way to All-American.

MOVE TO THE FRONT OF THE PACK

I loved basketball growing up and I also loved to run. If you watch any long-distance race, it seems like three groups of runners are generally formed. The leaders of the pack form the first group. The next group is the middle of the pack. The rest of the runners are at the back of the pack.

As you think about it, where would you place your child right now as an athlete? Is he a leader of the pack, in the middle of the pack, or at the back of the pack? Wherever he is, he may be content with his position and that is fine. However, if you feel he wants to improve his position you will have to help him understand that he has to practice on his own. He has to become his own coach. He will have to be willing to do what it takes to move to the front of the pack.

My hope is that the principles taught in this book will help you encourage your child to become his own coach. However, nothing taught on these pages will work unless your young athlete works. He must be, as the Bible says, a "doer of the word and not a hearer only." No coach, no parent, no friend can do it for your youngster. He must have a fire within him that will give him the self-discipline to follow the principles of the All-American Puzzle.

THERE IS NO OFF-SEASON

You need to help your child understand that the day after the last game of the season, the practices with teammates under the direction of the coach end, and the individual practices begin. It is during the off-season that individual skills are honed. Greatness is developed when a player coaches himself.

This individual development in the off-season does not end until retirement. Cycling legend Lance Armstrong said:

> If you asked me when I started preparing for the next Tour, my answer was, "The morning after." To my way of thinking, the Tour wasn't won in July; it was won by riding when other people weren't willing to.
>
> That meant there was no such thing as an off-season. I rode year-round. [1]

Discuss with your son what he plans to do during the next off-season to develop skills in preparation for the next season. Your youngster's off-season planning and the execution of his plans will be critical to his success.

During my basketball days I understood the principle of coaching myself. It was my self-discipline that always gave me hope as a player. I felt if I worked harder and played in more games than the rest of the guys in the off-season, then I would be that much further ahead when the next season started.

Bill Bradley, former All-American, NBA great, and U.S. Senator, said this about coaching himself:

> I couldn't get enough. If I hit 10 in a row, I wanted 15. If I hit 15, I wanted 25. Driven to excel by some deep . . . urge. I stayed out on that floor hour after hour, day after day, year after year. I played until my muscles stiffened and my arms ached. I persevered through blisters, contusions, and strained joints. When I got home I had to take a nap before I could muster the energy to eat the dinner that sat in the oven. After one Friday night high school game, which we lost to our arch-rival, I was back in the gym at eight on Saturday morning, with the bleachers still deployed and the popcorn boxes scattered beneath them, soaking my defeat by shooting. Others had been in this place last night, I thought, but now I was here by myself, and I was home. [2]

Why? Why did he do that? If he hit 15, why did he want 20? Why, when his "muscles stiffened and [his] arms ached," when he had "blisters, contusions and strained joints," why didn't he quit at the first sign of pain? Was his coach standing there forcing him on? Who was driving him? He was driving himself. His coach was there because he was coaching himself. He was on his way to becoming an All-American.

Evgeny Marchenko, coach of the amazing gymnast Carly Patterson said:

> What has gotten Carly so far? Her toughness, her motivation, and her discipline. She pushes herself very hard. She never lets go. Even in practice, if the last routine of the day doesn't work, Carly will keep at it until she gets it right. She can't bear to go to sleep knowing she has failed. Sometimes I can't kick her out of the gym. She'll be begging, "I want to do one more. I want to do one more." Her parents get upset because we have to wait while she overruns the practice time by an hour or an hour and a half. [3]

Carly Patterson is her own coach and a tough one at that.

SEEK OPPORTUNITIES TO PLAY

Without my junior high friend, Alex, I may not have ever made All-American. He and I spent two years together, from age 12 to 14. Our lives revolved around basketball in Louisville, Kentucky. We played one-on-one and all kinds of shooting games on my court. Whenever we could, we would go hunt for a game. Alex had an older brother who drove us to different city parks in Louisville where we got involved in some great pickup games.

Anything that related to basketball we did. Whenever there was a big game on television, we would have a pizza baking contest at his house before the game to see who could make the best pizza and then we would watch the game. After the game, we would go outside and try to duplicate some of the moves we had seen during the game.

We loved basketball. Anytime we could play ball, that's what we did. We even built ourselves a hoop that we could adjust up or down in six-inch increments from seven feet to ten feet. Our new hoop was located at the opposite end of the court from our normal hoop.

We spent many hours dunking the basketball on our "homemade" adjustable basket. I can't remember a time when I enjoyed basketball more. Without Alex it would have been difficult for me to have all that fun. I could play against my older brother, but that wasn't much fun because he or his buddies would kick me around.

Alex was the right friend at the right time for me. We played into the night on the lighted court by the side of my house, which was located on a very busy street. (We lost a few basketballs that bounced into the street and were run over by cars.)

As we played out there and enjoyed our time together, we had a dream that one day Denny Crum, then the coach of the University of Louisville basketball team, would drive by and see us. We dreamed he would pull over and ask us our names. He would offer us some tickets to a University of Louisville game and tell us that he would keep his eye on us as we got older.

Coach Crum never stopped to talk with us. He never saw us. But that didn't keep us from dreaming. It was five years later when Coach Crum sent one of his assistants halfway across the country to watch me play and offer me a scholarship when I was a high school senior. He could have had Alex and me signed and sealed a few years earlier.

ATTEND INSTRUCTIONAL CAMPS

As a young player, I loved attending sports camps, and over the years I have observed the different camps being offered to young people. There are some great camps and some not-so-great camps.

Before you enroll your son or daughter in a camp, ask the experienced parents in the community what camps they recommend. Usually the home-grown camps are better as far as individual attention and instruction goes. Area high school coaches will do a better job than most professional athletes because they will be able to spend more time with each child in the camp.

It is also a good idea to attend the camp of the coach of the high school where your child will be attending and to attend the neighboring high school coach's camp. One of the best basketball camps I went to as a young boy was directed by the coach of our high school's biggest rival. A primary benefit of attending sports camps is during the days preceding the camp, your child will be more motivated to practice to get ready for the camp. When the camp is over, he will be motivated to practice what he has learned.

At each camp I attended as a boy, I would learn a series of drills to do on my own. Then I would return home and be my own coach. After basketball camps, I would practice ball-handling drills, shooting drills, jumping drills, defensive drills, and more. There is no shortage of basketball drills a young person can do on his own. One of the beauties of basketball is that you really can have a good practice all by yourself. Unlike football or baseball, basketball gives you that opportunity.

Basketball camps were a source of great motivation for me. I would leave every camp feeling like there was hope for me to be a successful player. I was driven to go out and practice the things that were taught at these camps. However, the most important thing I got out of the basketball camps I attended was an increased desire to play and compete. If I could find a game—one-on-one, or five-on-five—that is where I would try to spend my time. As any young athlete knows there is not always a game ready to be played. If I couldn't find a game, I would work on drills I had learned at camp.

All skill development drills are good. The problem is that some drills become boring after a time. When playing by myself I would try to create some type of competitive situation. To coach myself, I needed to feel like I was making some progress. If I could make 17 out of 20 foul shots, I would keep shooting until I could make 18 out of 20. If I could make 20 jump shots from 15 feet in five minutes, then I would try to make the same amount of shots from the same spot in less time. When I was by myself, I always needed to create a competitive situation. Otherwise, my practices weren't that productive.

Along with group sports camps, you may find it beneficial to provide some individual instruction for your son and enlist the services of a local coach or an older player. These teachers can help your son hone his skills. They can teach him proper technique at a young age so that he won't have to break bad habits later on. They can also give encouragement and provide motivation. However, the primary benefit of individual instruction is an increase in your child's confidence.

SET HIGH GOALS

At the end of my freshman year at BYU, the basketball team met together before the summer break. The coaches challenged us to work hard over the summer and to prepare well for the following season. As part of the summer program, they asked each team member to make 20,000 shots. (For those of you who have ever tried to make 100 shots, you know that making 20,000 shots requires a tremendous effort.) They gave us some papers to use to chart our progress throughout the summer. They also challenged us to work on skill development, weightlifting, conditioning, and other things. However, the toughest challenge was to make that many shots. Sensing the enormity of the challenge, I looked around the room to observe the reaction of the other players. I could tell that not all were enthused about what they had been asked to do.

Summer passed and we came back to school that fall. Again, we were in a team meeting. The coaches asked us how our summers had gone and if we were able to work on the program they gave us. When asked for our sheets that documented our progress, only about half the guys still had these papers. The others, for one reason or another, had lost their progress charts although they reported they had shot a lot of shots and made much progress during the summer. Some players had actually charted their work and made the 20,000 shots. I am happy to report I was a member of that group. (My sisters, Kathryn and Marinda, did a lot of rebounding that summer. Thank you, ladies.)

For me, the thing that stood out in that meeting was when the coach asked a teammate, Mike Maxwell, how many shots he had made. Mike responded that he had made 100,000 shots over the summer. Everybody was stunned that Mike was able to make that many shots. If someone else had reported they had made 100,000 shots, I am sure no one would have believed him. But with Mike, if he said he made 100,000 shots, we all knew that he had done it. We knew of his integrity. Besides, he was one of the greatest shooters any of us had ever played with. Mike had been an All-American in high school and was on his way to becoming an All-American in college. Unfortunately, he suffered a serious knee injury that hampered what he was able to do during the rest of his college career.

Mike had grown up playing basketball. His dad was his high school coach and he had given him a desire to be a great basketball player. He had helped Mike develop a love of the game and a love for the gym. Mike had spent more hours in the gym than any of us had. However, the thing that made Mike great is he learned to coach himself. He did not need someone pushing him all the time. No one could push Mike harder than he pushed himself. Only if you push yourself harder than anyone else can push you, will you become the best you can be.

LIVE ABOVE THE LAW

Counsel your son to go beyond what is expected. I heard a story once about a young man who wanted to take a girl to a dance. He went to the door to pick up the girl and was invited inside by the girl's parents. Before they left, the father asked, "What time will you have my daughter home?"

"What time would you like her home?" the young man asked.

The father replied, "I'd like her home by midnight."

"Okay," the boy said. So they left and had a good time but the young man made sure the girl was home by 11:45 p.m.

Later he was asked by a friend, "Why did you take her home at 11:45? Why not stay out until midnight?" His reply was, "I wanted to live above the law."

Your son can apply that same principle when he is his own coach. A coach gives his players a set of things to do. He may ask them to run a mile a day. If your son lives above the law, he will run a mile and a half a day. A coach may ask his team to make 100 shots each day. Encourage your youngster to live above the law and make 150. Help your child establish a high standard for himself. By living above the law, a player will improve at a faster rate.

When your son loves doing something, he does not need somebody telling him to do it all the time. He wants to do it. If there is a game out there he will want to find it. He enjoys shooting baskets. He likes hanging out with his neighborhood friend, playing one-on-one hour after hour, and playing other skill-development games that will help him be a better basketball player. He has always got someone to play one-on-one with. That is when basketball is probably its most fun—when it is just a boy and his buddy out looking for games or competing against each other.

A great coach is going to do all he can to have a disciplined team. However, the team's success only comes when each player is able to discipline or coach himself.

The master of disciplining himself and living above the law is Lance Armstrong. He tells this story of a cycling workout:

> The weather was blustery and I rode the exact route we would take, only there were no spectators and I was alone except for Johan in a follow car. I arrived at the foot of Hautacam, and I began to jog atop the pedals, working my way up the steep hillside. I studied the road as I went, trying to decide where I might attack, and where I'd need to save myself. It was pouring down a mixture of snow and sleet, and my breath streamed out in a white vapor.
>
> After about an hour, I reached the top. Johan pulled up and stuck his head out of the car window. "Okay, good. Get in the car and have some hot tea," he said. I hesitated. I was unhappy about the way I'd ridden.
>
> "I didn't get it," I said.
>
> "What do you mean you didn't get it?"
>
> "I didn't get it. I don't understand the climb."
>
> A mountain could be a complicated thing. I didn't feel like I knew Hautacam. I'd climbed it, but I was still uncertain about how to pace myself up it. At the end of a rehearsed climb, I wanted to feel that I knew the mountain so well that it might help me.
>
> "I don't think I know it," I said. "It's not my friend."
>
> "What's the problem?" he said. "You got it, let's go."
>
> "We're going to have to go back and do it again."

It had taken an hour to get up, and it took about 30 minutes to get back down. And then I rode it again, straight up for another hour. This time, at the end of the day, in the driving rain, when I was done, I felt I'd mastered the climb. At the top, Johan met me with a raincoat. "I don't believe what I just saw," he said.

"All right. Now let's go home." [4]

I love that story about a champion coaching himself to greatness. It's little wonder that Lance Armstrong has achieved the level of excellence he has.

ALWAYS GIVE YOUR BEST EFFORT

Between my junior and senior years of high school, I went to a basketball camp at BYU. On the next to last day there was a three-on-three competition. The two other guys on my team were on their way to major college basketball programs. We figured we would win the three-on-three competition without much effort. On the day of our game, the BYU coaching staff took us out to a nice Mexican lunch. We ate a lot of rice and beans and tortillas. As soon as we arrived back at the gym we had to play a three-on-three game against three guys from Richfield, Utah, a rural community. We thought we would make quick work of these farm boys whose basketball days would end with high school. That did not happen. As we started playing, we began to feel our lunch. Those farm boys proceeded to beat us good.

We didn't want to, but we still had to compete in the losers bracket. We had lost our chance to win because we had taken the first game lightly, ate too much, and had not properly prepared. We really didn't put much effort into our second game because we were playing in the losers bracket. We were losers again.

Afterward, my high school coach, Jim Spencer, was very upset with me. He told me in no uncertain terms that what I had done was wrong. He told me that I had played half-heartedly in the losers competition and he emphatically announced, "Whenever a player competes, his opponent deserves that player's best effort." I will never forget that lesson.

A hallmark of a successful team coach is that he plans and carries out productive and intense practices. He makes sure everything is done correctly in order to improve his team's play in games.

Your child, acting as his own coach, must do the same. He cannot just put in the time in a haphazard and lackadaisical manner. Personal practice time is not a time for goofing off. It is a time to go at game speed and intensity—at least as much as possible.

During those times when your son has to coach himself, he might not feel like giving his best effort. Give him extra support during those times. Let him know you believe in him and encourage him to work harder. If he is practicing by himself, teach him that he deserves to give himself his best effort. If he is competing against someone else, his opponent deserves his best effort.

We all know that when the coach comes into the gym, those playing in a pickup game suddenly become much more intense and determined in their play. Teach your son in personal practice that he must act as though his coach is watching and ask himself, "What is the coach thinking of how I am playing today? Right now?" Then remind him that he is his own coach, and for that reason he should expect his best effort from himself.

PRACTICE PERFECT

Coach Spencer and Coach Frank Arnold, my BYU coach, were sticklers on making the most of each practice session. Coach Arnold would tell us, "Practice doesn't make perfect. Perfect practice makes perfect." He would insist that we do a skill correctly and then repeat it over and over again until it became natural for us to do it correctly.

Bill Bradley says this about one of the greatest big men to ever play the game:

> Kareem, the league MVP for the previous two seasons, was already on the floor practicing, shooting skyhook after skyhook, perfecting his graceful release, grooving his rhythm—look at the basket, step left, cradle the ball, right leg up, swing the right arm high, release, follow through—putting in the time as if he were a sophomore in high school. To Kareem, this effort at skill development was just part of being a champion. An aspect of his daily routine involved shooting the hook with a rebounding ring inside the rim, thereby shrinking the space available for a successful shot. When he removed the ring after the thirty-day training periods, he said that he felt as if he were shooting the ball into the ocean."

The skyhook Kareem perfected through many hours of practice became the most powerful offensive weapon the sport of basketball has ever known. Many observers who saw these sweet hook shots swish though the nets to win games thought they all came naturally. Not so. That which came naturally to Kareem were the endless hours of correct practice.

Encourage your son to choose a skill or move he desires to perfect and have him work on it until it becomes a part of him. As a father, make it easy for your child to coach himself. Make sure he has the tools needed to be a good self-coach. Make it convenient for your son to go out and work on his game by himself or with a friend.

CONVERT WEAKNESSES INTO STRENGTHS

My Uncle Bill was a junior high physical education teacher. He had a ninth grader in his class named Dick Nemelka, who went on to become a college All-American at BYU. In the ninth grade gym class basketball games, my Uncle Bill would make Dick tie his right hand to his side so he couldn't use it. This forced Dick to develop his ability to use his left hand. He became so good, under this restriction, he was soon able to continue to dominate the games using only his left hand.

Ask your child, "Are you only good with one hand? Can you defend well? What do you feel are your weaknesses?" Then encourage your child to work on the areas of his game that need improvement. Help him convert weaknesses into strengths.

A great quote to remember is this one, often attributed to Ralph Waldo Emerson: "That which we persist in doing becomes easier for us to do—not that the nature of the thing is changed, but that our power to do it is increased."

A basketball player can make his left hand as good as his right if he persists in using it. Are your child's hands so weak that an opponent can rip the basketball away from him? Get him a hand gripper and encourage him to make his hands so strong that no one can take the ball from him.

When Los Angeles defeated Boston in a playoff series in the 1980s it was in part because Michael Cooper, a defensively gifted player, held Boston Celtic legend Larry Bird in check. After the defeat, Larry analyzed what had happened:

> Saying the Lakers were better didn't make it much easier to take. But once I decided that this was the case, the next question was: What can I do to get better? The first thing I decided was that I needed to work on my left hand. Whenever I'm trying to improve my game, I analyze my weaknesses first and work on those relentlessly. When Cooper made all those subtle changes on me, I knew I needed to come up with something new. [6]

A future All-American's school coach can point out his weaknesses, but he can't correct them. That is up to the athlete, and the off-season is the time to do it. As your son practices, encourage him to shoot the type of shots he will shoot in a game. It is good to be a good defender and a good ball handler, but it sure is a plus if your child can put the ball in the basket. A player learns to shoot by shooting. Help your youngster to concentrate on bending the knees, positioning the elbow, flicking the wrist, and following through. Encourage him to do it right and then to repeat it over and over again.

By the time a player reaches the professional level he may have shot a basketball at a hoop a million times. I wonder how many shots a player has taken by the time he graduates from high school? Let's see, how many did my college teammate hit in a summer? 100,000. I can't imagine a high schooler has ever done that. But if your child decides to be his own coach, and if he keeps a record, he could hit 20,000 shots a summer from the ninth grade on. That would add up to a lot of shots by the time he was a senior. Something happens in a player's mind when he sees the ball going into the basket so many times. He starts to believe that every shot should go in. That's the kind of confidence you want your son to feel.

Encourage your child to make a lot of shots and keep track with a written shooting record. It will pay off. Bill Bradley describes how two great shooters pushed themselves during their playing days:

> Chris Mullin, with two assistants feeding him balls, regularly takes an incredible one thousand shots in a normal one-hour practice. In 1984, Larry Bird was the league MVP and the leader of the world-champion Boston Celtics. Shortly after the celebrations ended, he went home to French Lick, Indiana. All summer he lifted weights in the morning and for hours every afternoon went to a gym, often alone, and shot baskets. Magic Johnson once said of Larry Bird, "To most players, basketball is a job. To Larry, it was life." [7]

My sisters were good enough to do a lot of rebounding for me over the years. My wife became my rebounder in the later years and now helps my sons by rebounding for them. A faithful rebounder, while not a necessity, is certainly a plus for anyone who wants to be a great shooter.

NO SUN IN THE GYM

One of the greatest shooters to play the game of basketball was Kiki Vandeweghe. During our college days, Kiki and I were teammates on a United States team that competed in China. An All-American at UCLA, Kiki led his team to the NCAA title his senior year. He went on to a stellar career in the NBA and now is the general manager of the Denver Nuggets. I heard a story about Kiki that I'm not sure is true but it makes a great point. The story goes that someone asked Kiki one day why his legs were so white. His response was a classic. He said, "My legs are so white because I'm always in the gym and the sun doesn't shine in the gym."

Kiki could have been distracted by a number of things—as is the case with any young athlete, but he was focused on improving his game in any way he could and he was willing to put in the time to do it.

While I'm on the subject of distractions, my wife and I have gone to great lengths to limit video games, television, and internet time in our house. Today's numerous digital entertainment options can be a huge distraction that athletes of the past didn't have to deal with. Help your son or daughter enjoy the advances in technology in moderation. Excess entertainment will deter a pursuit of excellence.

KEEP RAISING THE BAR

On the night the Los Angeles Lakers received their championship rings from the season before, they were humiliated by the lowly (at that time) Cleveland Cavaliers. The

Laker players had been told before the game that they had to get better than they had been the year before. To this challenge from Coach Pat Riley, one of the players said:

> "Coach, we whipped Boston in their own building [last year] . . . How do you expect us to top what we did last year?" . . . We got taught a simple truth: anytime you stop striving to get better, you're bound to get worse. There's no such thing in life as simply holding on to what you've got.[8]

Coach Rick Pitino adds this advice to those who are satisfied with past accomplishments:

> . . . the people who will ultimately pull ahead and wind up on top are the ones who . . . keep raising the bar, becoming neither discouraged by pitfalls nor complacent by success. They understand that the pursuit of excellence is a marathon, not a sprint. It is a journey, not some little day trip.[9]

Pat Williams tells of a conversation between Michael Jordan and his college coach, Dean Smith, that illustrates Jordan's desire to improve or "raise the bar":

> Coach Smith at North Carolina reminded him that defense won games. So Jordan worked on his defense and eventually became the best defensive player in the NBA. Every pickup game, every practice, was an opportunity to improve, to polish the weaker aspects of his game. There was always room to improve.[10]

IT'S WORTH IT

Next year when the starting lineup is chosen is not the time to take the game seriously. The time to get ready is now. Your child must, while he is his own coach, feel as though he has earned his place on the team and on the sports page.

As Coach Pitino said:

> It is not always going to be fun. It is not always going to happen for you overnight. . . . As a coach I'm always trying to explain to my players that all the pain they're going through is worth it. That there's a great reward for them if they keep at it. I must keep explaining to them how special the payoff is going to be for them at the end. Only then are they going to be able to get through those moments when they hit the wall and want to quit.[11]

CHOOSE GOOD ATHLETIC ROLE MODELS

Encourage your son to find an athlete to model his game after. Somebody who motivates him to do all he can to someday play the way his favorite athlete plays.

As a young boy I spent hundreds of hours imagining that I was Julius Erving. Years passed and I found myself playing for the Indiana Pacers. One night my team was playing against the Philadelphia 76ers; I was actually playing on the same court with my boyhood idol—Julius Erving. I even got to guard my hero. I was bumping him and doing all I could to contain him. At one point he said to the official, "Get this guy off me." I was very tempted to walk up to Julius and say, "Whatever you want, you can have because you have been my hero for many years. It is an honor to be on the same court with you. If I'm pushing and fouling and you'd like me to back off, then that's what I'll do. Thank you, Mr. Erving." What a privilege it was for me to be competing against my hero and one of the all-time greats— Julius Erving!

When we moved to Kentucky my older brother played for Seneca High School. There was a big guy on that team named Wayne Cosby. I was amazed as I watched his games and saw him, a six-foot-six guy, bringing the ball down the court against the press. He had a nice reverse spin dribble. He would come to one defender, reverse pivot and leave his defender standing alone, go to the next guy and do the same. To me it was incredible how he could do that. I dreamed of being able to handle the ball the way he did. I practiced dribbling drills for hours because of Wayne Cosby. Later as a six-foot-seven-inch high school forward, I was often called upon to bring the ball up the court against the press.

When I wasn't pretending that I was Julius Erving or Wayne Cosby, I was playing as if I was Darrell Griffith. He was a high school player during my junior high days in Louisville, Kentucky. I wish all young basketball players could enjoy the great times that my friend Alex and I had following Darrell Griffith throughout his high school years. He was a tremendously gifted athlete and a terrific person.

CHOOSE GOOD CHARACTER ROLE MODELS

Counsel your son that it is good to choose a character role model as well as an athletic role model. Maybe the two will be the same person. But if not, there should be plenty of people for your son to choose from when looking for a good character role model. My primary character role model was my father. I can't say that my Dad is perfect but he is as close to it as anyone I have ever known. Maybe your son admires a teacher, a church leader, or another adult who lives an exemplary life. Encourage your son to incorporate into his own life the values he sees in those he admires.

Discuss with your youngster how, as he works towards excellence in athletics, he can use the same principles he is using to excel as an athlete to excel in other areas of his life. He can be a good student by coaching himself academically. He can get his homework done before mom or dad has to encourage him to do it. He can be a good citizen. He can be friendly at home to the family and at school to his classmates.

Help your child understand that it is all right if he is not on the school honor roll. However, it is not all right if his grades are a disgrace. I am always pleased to hear of a great athlete who is also an honor student. I am dismayed to hear of a great one who is academically ineligible. Encourage your child to avoid being known as a "dumb jock." Instead, instill in him a desire to want to be known as a scholar as well as an athlete.

PRACTICE SELF-DISCIPLINE

Some have the talent, but they lack the self-discipline needed to become an All-American. They can't coach themselves. Of this Charles Barkley said:

> We could sit here and talk about basketball stuff, but it's the management of your life that is really the big difference between making it and not making it for a lot of guys, or hanging on versus making it big. If you don't start with that, you're wasting your time. I've probably played with 20 players who should have played in the NBA for a long time but didn't. It's because their heads weren't together. You see guys with talent all the time who can't make it.[12]

MAINTAIN PROPER BALANCE IN LIFE

As your son coaches himself, make sure he has balance in his life. Help him understand that his chosen pursuit is going to take a huge time commitment. However, this does not mean that he need not have other goals and responsibilities in life outside of sports. Help him to never lose sight of the fact that a sports career is going to end sooner than he would probably think. Tell him to remember that as he pursues his athletic dream to take time to improve his life in other areas. Help him decide what those other areas might be. For my children, balance in life is provided by piano lessons, church service, scout programs, and other academic pursuits. Balance also comes from allowing children to be responsible for their share of the work around the house.

TAKE GOOD CARE OF YOUR BODY

Teach your son the significance of taking care of his body and the importance of proper diet and exercise. Teach him to avoid harmful substances at all costs. His body is the vehicle that will take him to success. That vehicle has to be maintained in top condition at all times.

When Charles Barkley was younger, his role model was John Drew. John Drew was a terrific offensive basketball player. He was a two-time NBA All-Star. Years later when Sir Charles left an arena after a game he ran into a destitute person on the street asking for money. Later Barkley realized that the down-and-out man was John Drew. He had ruined his life by misusing alcohol and drugs. Examples are numerous of athletes who had the ability, yet they did not have enough self-discipline to take proper care of their bodies.

PRACTICE PERFECT GAME DAY PREPARATION

Game day preparation will be different for each player. Your child should begin now to experiment to see if he plays better or worse by eating or drinking this or that at this time or that time. When he gets good results, he'll want to repeat that pattern. It has often been said, if you keep doing what you are doing you will keep getting what you are getting. If you don't like today's results, try something different.

As I got older, what seemed to work best for me on game day was to eat four hours before game time. I would usually have a chicken breast and a baked potato. I always drank water with my meal. I liked to be feeling just a little hungry at game time. If you can taste your pre-game meal as you warm up, you didn't eat early enough.

MAKE THE FIRE HOT

I mentioned earlier that I have an interest in real estate. Recently, I decided to develop the orchard behind my house into building lots. That meant cutting down trees and burning some limbs. One Saturday I went out to a stack of limbs, lit some lower twigs with some newspaper and waited for the limbs to burn. They smoked a little and then went out. I tried again but I couldn't get the limbs to burn because of the moisture in the wood.

The next weekend I took some gasoline out there to pour onto the limbs. Then I threw a match on the gas-soaked limbs. Initially, there was a burst of flames. But almost as suddenly as it started, it ended. I considered the situation and concluded I was not generating enough heat for that fire to burn the moist wood. I put some dry wood at the base and put the moist wood on top and lit the fire again. By doing that I was finally able to get a good fire going. At that point, I could throw on all the wood that I wanted—dry or green—and it would burn. I had finally generated enough heat for the flames to sustain themselves without any more help from me.

That is analogous to what you might have to do with your son. There may be times when you have to get a fire burning within him. It is best to do this when your child is young. Once the fire is burning hot, it is not going to take much additional motivation from you because he will be putting on his own wood to keep the fire burning. Once the fire is burning hot, just stand back, enjoy the warmth, and cheer for your youngster.

HELP HIM ORDER FROM HIS OWN MENU

For three years in college, I was coached by Frank Arnold.

He had served as an assistant to the legendary John Wooden for several years. Coach Arnold was a man of details. His hope was to gain every advantage possible over the opponent by paying attention to each detail.

His concern for detail even extended to the pre-game meal. We always had a steak, green beans, a fruit cup, a baked potato, and water. There were no variations. We were also given a small piece of butter for the potato and a minimum amount of ice to cool our water. Coach Arnold found that this food combination had been successful for him and the players he had worked with over the years. A lot of things changed in the world during those three years under Coach Arnold but one thing that never changed was what the BYU Cougars ate for their pre-game meal.

I will never forget the first road game of my senior year with new coach Ladell Andersen. We were in Logan to play against Utah State. We sat down for the pre-game meal, and in front of each of us was a menu. We were all confused because we were waiting for our steak, baked potato, green beans, and fruit cup to be placed before us.

Looking at Coach, I said, "What are the menus for?" He replied, "What do you mean, what are menus for? Don't you know how to order from a menu?"

Sure I did. But not for a pre-game meal. That was not an option for me in past years. Then I realized that what he was saying was we were to choose for ourselves. He was saying, "Isn't it about time you started coaching yourself? You know what you need to eat before a game. If you don't know by now you'd better figure it out. Open the menu and order what you think is the best food for you to eat before the game."

While I didn't mind Coach Arnold's approach—he used his experience to help his players—this new coach was saying, "You need to use your own experience to figure out what is going to be the best pre-game meal for you." There was a great lesson for me in that experience.

PLAY MULTIPLE SPORTS

Perhaps your child's athletic menu should go beyond the sport in which he desires to excel. As your youngster grows up, encourage him to participate in as many sports as possible—basketball in the winter, baseball in the spring and summer, and football or other sports in the fall. Obviously, your child will be under the direction of various coaches as he competes in different sports. However, his desire to be fully involved will be because he is acting as his own coach and wants to improve his overall strength, agility, speed, endurance, and mental toughness. When the time comes to compete in his chosen sport, he will be better prepared to succeed.

You may ask yourself, "If I want my son to be a basketball player, what benefit is there in having him play baseball?" Baseball will develop his hand-eye coordination. He will learn how to work within the framework of a team. One of the most important things he will learn is how to deal with pressure. While playing baseball, he will feel a lot of pressure when he is at the plate as the spectators, his teammates, and the coaching staff watch him. All eyes will be on him. He has to produce. Later, he is going to be at the foul line and again spectators, teammates, and coaches will be watching him. If he can deal with pressure, he will make the big foul shot to win the game.

I would suggest that any male basketball player play football because he will learn what it is like to take a hit and the importance of being able to be physically competitive. As a youngster, I loved to play tackle football. I believe it made me a better hoopster. Sometimes I regret not having played organized football past the seventh grade. Basketball is becoming more and more physical all the time. If your son is uncomfortable getting hit, he is going to have a hard time driving hard to the basket, going up in the air, and being knocked around by other players. Football will prepare him for that kind of thing.

The reverse is also true. Playing basketball will benefit a football player. If a good basketball player plays wide receiver on the football team, he will do well. He will have a better chance at running down the field 20 yards, going up in the air, and catching a pass from the quarterback than will someone else who has not played basketball. That is because he is comfortable being up in the air doing things with a ball.

I am a big believer in the importance of conditioning. I think basketball players should seriously consider joining the track or cross-country team to develop endurance and lung capacity. It is another way to keep in shape during the off-season. Ever since I can remember, I have loved to run. I never joined the cross-country team in high school but I wish I would have. I found great satisfaction (and pain) in racing against my teammates in college as we went through our pre-season conditioning work.

WORK WHILE THE COMPETITION IS RESTING

No matter how many sports your son plays under the direction of coaches, there is still much downtime after each day's organized practice.

Recently, I spoke with the father of a young female runner who is making a mark in international circles as a distance runner. He told me that many times after the college team practice ends, his daughter will come home and go out behind her house and run in the foothills. She loves to run in the foothills and is on her way to becoming an All-American because of her tremendous self-discipline.

I like the idea of your daughter or son being their "own coach." However, a synonymous term is being his or her own "disciplinarian." To me these two concepts are really one. It will do no good for your child to have a menu if he does not have the self-discipline to make good choices. Your youngster must do it on his own. If you find that you are always the one encouraging your son to go shoot, to go play, to eat right and get enough sleep, then it is your flame that is burning, not his. Such a child still has not learned to coach himself or it may be that he lacks the desire. We'll discuss lack of desire in Part Seven. On the other hand, once you see he is taking those steps on his own, when there is no one else around, then be sure to give your child the needed positive reinforcement—fan the flame.

I loved the endless hours when I acted as my own coach. However, it was my other coaches who, in the little time they had with me, helped give me a desire and a plan so I could coach myself in their absence.

No coach can do the total job, or even most of the job, of helping an athlete to be all that he or she can be. Tell your child that it is up to him, to say "If it is to be, it is up to me." And it can only be if he has the strict self-discipline to do what he will need to do when he is on his own.

Consider the words of tennis legend, John McEnroe, on being his own coach:

> . . . to tell you the truth, I've always been my own best coach. Sometimes it got lonely, but a lot of the time I didn't mind being by myself.[13]

Help your son become his own best coach. You will have more to do with your child becoming an All-American than anyone other than your son. He will have to do the work. However, it will be you who will influence him to have the self-discipline to coach himself. Only he who learns that valuable trait will become an All-American in sports and a winner in life.

DEVIN DURRANT'S
ALL-AMERICAN PUZZLE

PART 3
BE COACHABLE

HELP YOUR YOUNG ATHLETE TO BE COACHABLE

It does no good to have a coach like Rick Bolus if your child is not coachable. When I look back to the time when I played for Coach Bolus, the main factor that made that time so valuable for me was that I was coachable. When Coach Bolus spoke I tried to look directly into his eyes. When he asked me to do something, I replied, "Sir, yes sir!" Whatever he asked of me, I was determined to do it. I did not always like what he asked me to do, but I did it anyway because I believed that it would make me a better basketball player. When he taught us defense, I tried my best to do as he taught. When he taught us our offense, I did my best to follow his instructions and make the offense work. I knew that he was the coach and that he was in charge. I was one of his players and I did as he said. I certainly had my days when I wondered why he demanded so much of us. Nevertheless, I did as I was told. Occasionally, I would tell my Dad how hard practice was and how mean Coach Bolus was, but I never asked for sympathy or for pity. Fortunately, he never interfered. I think my Dad knew Coach Bolus was good for me and his quiet influence helped me be coachable.

From those junior high days until I ended my career as a basketball player, I tried to be coachable. I knew each coach I played for could offer me some puzzle pieces I could interlock in one of the nine parts of my All-American Puzzle. I was determined not to miss out on a single piece.

BE TEACHABLE

Coachable and teachable are synonymous. Coaches are first and foremost, teachers. Players are students. When speaking or teaching, every coach likes a player who looks him in the eye and nods to acknowledge understanding and agreement. Coaches wonder about players who look back at them in a challenging way. They don't know if the player is willing to do what he has been asked to do.

Coaches want to feel players care about what they say. It is an insult to ignore them. During practice, during timeouts, in the post-game, etc., a coachable player will give his coach his undivided attention and then do what he has been told to do. If the coach tells the team he wants them to make five passes before a shot is taken, a coachable player listens and does what the coach says.

If the coach wants the team to press after made foul shots, a coachable player remembers the instruction. If the coach says to get the ball into the low post, a player should not shoot a "three" at the first opportunity. A coachable player listens to the coach and obeys him. That is always the best policy, but sometimes it is most critical. If during a last second time out, a coach tells a player to come off a screen and instead, the player sets a screen, that mistake could cost the team the game.

If a player doesn't learn to listen, then he will have to learn to like a seat on the bench. Help your son remember that more opportunities come to those who are willing to be taught.

THE FANCY PASS

When I was a freshman playing for Brigham Young University, Coach Arnold did not like behind-the-back passes or any kind of fancy pass and he told us so. I remember vividly the time when I caught the ball on a fast break and a defender caused me to stop and turn my back to the basket. As my teammates came running down the floor, no one in the first wave was open.

Then I noticed our center, Alan Taylor, who was trailing the play, running down the floor toward our basket. I was at the foul line extended, and Alan ran up the opposite side of the lane and was headed unguarded directly for the basket. So with my back to our basket, I threw the ball behind my head, trying to hit Alan for an easy lay-up or dunk. The only problem with my plan was that as I released the ball toward my teammate, the guy who was guarding me deflected it to one of his teammates who took off with the ball the other way. At the next dead ball, Coach Arnold took me out of the game. When I walked off the court he let me know, in no uncertain terms, that was the last fancy pass I would ever throw behind my head.

Sitting on the bench, I had to make a decision. I could shout back at my coach. I could pout and say to myself, "He is wrong." I could go back in the game and ignore his instructions. Or, I could follow the coach's direction and eliminate the behind-the-head pass from my game. I liked playing. I hated sitting on the bench. So I didn't want to do anything to alienate my coach. That was the last behind the head pass that I remember throwing in my college career or my professional career. I was permanently cured.

This amusing anecdote about NBA great Allen Iverson is a lesson for young players who get tired of their coach's instructions. At the time of this account, Allen was a sophomore in high school:

As [Allen] played point guard, his basketball coach constantly yelled instructions to him. "Allen! Pass the ball ahead!" Finally Iverson wheeled around at mid-court and shouted, "Coach! Stop telling me how to play all the time!"

Coach Bailey benched him and kept him there through the third and fourth quarters even though it cost his team the game. It was an uncharacteristic move on Bailey's part; he was not known to be stern when it came to Iverson. Walking off, Bailey approached his star.

"Do you like me not coaching you?" he asked. "It's real easy when you're sitting on the end of the bench for me to not say much to you."[1]

CHANGE YOURSELF RATHER THAN TRYING TO CHANGE THE COACH

One of the things that has always amazed me as a basketball player is how much time some players spend wishing the coach would change the way he did things—wishing that the coach would change the offense, wishing that the coach would change the defense, wishing the coach would change who he plays. Those players need to take all that energy and think about what they can change within themselves. A potential All-American doesn't worry about the things he can't control. He just deals with the things he can control. As a player, one thing he can control is where he is going to expend his energy. An athlete should focus on how to become a better athlete. A coachable athlete will try to understand what the coach is trying to accomplish and then do his best to make that happen.

RESPECT THE COACHES

At times, it may appear a coach is not too knowledgeable. Maybe a junior high math teacher is assigned by the principal to coach, and he doesn't seem to know much about the sport.

Nevertheless, a player's job is to do what the coach tells him to do. As time passes, even an ill-informed coach will learn about the game and he may be able to give some helpful tips. Every coach can offer some good instruction that might help a player if that player is not set on being critical of him.

As I mentioned earlier, I lived three years in the South. While living there, I was taught to address my elders with "Yes sir" and "Yes ma'am." Every sentence we spoke to Coach Bolus in practice began and ended with the word, "sir."

We called him "sir" because we had to at first, but over time we called him "sir" because he deserved our respect. It is amazing what a good coach can do for a player who will allow himself to be taught.

Some athletes find it easy to be coachable when the head coach is talking, but when the assistant coach speaks, they don't show the same amount of respect to him or her. Don't make that mistake. Assistant coaches help the head coach make important decisions. They help make playing time decisions. They can give a player ideas on how to improve his game. A player should show the same amount of respect and courtesy to assistant coaches as he does to the head coach.

THE IMPACT OF A GOOD COACH

I enjoy hearing stories of the great players as they look back on some of their earliest coaches. Larry Bird said this of the instruction he received from his high school coach:

> I went out for the high school basketball team and made the B team. Fortunately for me, Jim Jones was the coach. Coach Jones is the man I have to thank for drumming basketball fundamentals into my head. He taught me every basic maneuver there is and once he would show me something, it would just seem to click in my mind. It didn't matter what it was: a reverse pivot, boxing out, getting rebounds, whatever. Coach Jones

taught me to utilize my left hand as well as my right. Once he told me that, I began to practice dribbling full-court with my left hand and I was amazed at how quickly my left hand adjusted.

. . . Once I started getting seriously interested in basketball, I listened when Jonesie [his coach] told me something. A lot of kids still let it all go in one ear and out the other, but I've been blessed with a good memory and I was able to remember every piece of instruction.[2]

Follow Larry Bird's example and do your best to remember every piece of instruction offered by your coach.

COACHES LOVE THEIR PLAYERS— MOST OF THE TIME

Some athletes say, "The coach doesn't like me." That attitude creates a self-imposed negative barrier blocking the athlete from success. Remember a coach usually loves his players because they are playing their guts out for him. A coach may criticize a player, but that doesn't mean he doesn't like the player. The coach wants to win. If a team member helps him do that, he will treat that player like a son because that player is helping him succeed.

Generally speaking, if the coach seems to not like a player, it is because the player is not doing the things that will help the team win. A potential All-American doesn't blame his lack of playing time on a feeling that the coach doesn't like him personally.

The coach is going to play those players that he thinks give him the best chance to get a victory. So if your son blames his lack of minutes on the coach not liking him, help your son to work harder to improve his game and to be more coachable. If your son does his part, it's likely he'll start to feel that the coach really does like him.

IT IS OKAY TO DISLIKE AND/OR FEAR THE COACH

Some coaches are a lot easier to hate than to love. Despising a coach at times is okay. It can be a release for you or your son. That is the way it was for me with Coach Bolus. Keep in mind that an unlikable coach might be the key to future athletic success.

Help your child recognize that a coach's rantings may be his way of telling a player that he cares enough to want his young athlete to do his best. It is not pleasant to be yelled at for having made a mistake but it is the coach's job to push the player. If he says, "You'll never get 10 rebounds in a game because you aren't tough enough," a potential All-American will show the coach he is wrong by getting more than 10 rebounds.

A player won't generally have positive feelings toward a coach who at times is critical of him, but his feelings may change over time. A coach has to be a little crazy, even mean at times. He may have to yell and rant and rave in order to get a player to perform at his best.

Some coaches use the fear factor to motivate and teach their players. One of the most successful college coaches ever, Bob Knight, used fear to help his team win:

> This was Knight's basic coaching philosophy. Beyond all the talk about his complexity, his fundamental approach to motivation has never changed: fear is his number one weapon. He believes that if the players are afraid of getting screamed at or of landing in the doghouse, they will play better. And, if they fear him more than the opponent, they are likely to play better.[3]

Not all coaches use the fear factor as vigorously as does Coach Knight but many coaches at times will use it. It is okay to fear a coach. Help your son overcome his fear of the coach by helping him understand that the coach is simply using fear as a tool to motivate his team to improve.

LEARN AND ADOPT THE COACH'S PHILOSOPHY

Is your coach a stickler for discipline on offense, or does he allow some degree of freedom? Encourage your athlete to get to know the coach—what he will and will not allow—and to play within the parameters of the coach's system.

Coaches are not all the same so a player must adjust to each one as he comes along. A junior high coach may have a different style than a high school coach. A coachable player doesn't wish all coaches were the same. He just takes the pieces each offers and puts them into his puzzle. He then moves on to the next coach and makes the adjustments that his teaching style demands. Of two of his coaches, Bill Bradley wrote:

> My coach at Princeton was Bill (Butch) Van Breda Koff. We didn't have very many set plays. There were no drills for passing or boxing out on rebounds. He taught us about the fundamentals in the context of play, stopping a half-court or full-court game from time to time to tell us what we could have done better. Under his freelance offense, players developed the ability to create, to see things emerging. Above all, the game was fun. My coach for the 1964 Olympics, Hank Iba of Oklahoma State, took the opposite approach. Every morning during practice, he lectured the team, using a blackboard to display diagrams for the offense. We had to keep notebooks of these lectures. During a game, he tolerated no deviation from his plays or their options. Both coaches emphasized conditioning. Their personalities and their styles of coaching were as different as their preferred offenses, but both men engendered respect—Van Breda Koff because of his intensity in competition, Iba because of his thoroughness in practice.[4]

NO EXCUSES

Athletics can provide us with plenty of opportunities to make excuses because there are plenty of opportunities to make mistakes. Whenever a player makes a mistake there is an opportunity to make an excuse. A coachable player is not an excuse maker. He takes responsibility for his actions. If his coach takes him out and jumps all over him, he doesn't blame the coach. He is accountable for his own errors. When he makes a mistake, he acknowledges it and moves on. He then does his best not to make the same mistake again.

MY LONG NAP

I remember well a big mistake I made when I was a sophomore in high school and I was playing on the junior varsity team. Before one game I decided to take a brief nap. For one reason or another, my alarm didn't go off at the appointed time. When I woke up I looked at the clock and I saw that my game was scheduled to start in fifteen minutes. I lived a couple of blocks away from the school so I got up and ran out the door as fast as I could. I ran all the way to the gym. When I arrived, I opened the locker room door, and there were all my teammates and my coach, Coach Coombs.

My teammates were about two minutes away from going out onto the court for the opening tip. Coach Coombs said, "I'll bet your sundial worked better in Kentucky than it does here in Utah." I appreciated that he used humor to defuse my embarrassment. However, because I was late, he punished me. I didn't get to play in the first quarter although normally I was a starter. I got to sit the bench and pay for my actions. I didn't blame the coach. It was my own fault that I was being punished. Finally, Coach Coombs put me in the game in the second quarter. We went on to win the game and all was forgotten. The coach didn't continue to make me pay for my mistake and we moved forward.

Excuses can be the biggest deterrent to an athlete's growth. Don't let your child specialize in excuses, and do your best to not make excuses for him. Help him take responsibility for his game and for himself.

If I had been late as a professional player, my coach might have fined me and taken a portion of my paycheck. A high school coach can't fine a player with money, but he can fine him in other ways. However, the big fine that comes from making excuses is the fine that happens inside the player and causes him to be less than he could be if he just took responsibility for his own actions and left the excuses behind.

TAKE CRITICISM AND MOVE ON

A coachable player knows he needs to take criticism or he will never get any better. One thing all great players seem to have in common is during their careers, one or more coaches were critical of them. As a matter of fact, one common method of coaching is criticism.

One of the best examples I have ever seen of someone who could take criticism and then go out and do good things was Charles Barkley. I was his teammate representing the United States in the University Games in 1983. As we prepared for the games, we spent some time in Kansas City where we played an exhibition game.

At one point in the game I was on the bench and Charles was on the floor. He made a mistake and the coach immediately sent someone in for him. Charles came over to the bench and sat down right by me. Our coach, Norm Stewart, who was the coach at the University of Missouri at the time, walked down the bench and stood above where the two of us were seated. I don't remember what Charles had done wrong on the court, but Coach Stewart let him have it. I watched Charles as he looked Coach in the eye. He didn't say anything, didn't challenge him, just took it like a man.

Coach Stewart finished his tirade, returned to his chair, and sat down. Charles got himself ready to go back in the game. Nothing more was said of it. It was over for Charles and it was over for Coach Stewart. Charles went on and had a successful experience with that team at the University Games.

I was impressed at how well Charles handled that tongue lashing. It took a lot of character just to take it and move on, but I believe Charles knew Coach Stewart's goal was to make him a better player.

Later in his life Barkley said:

> Young guys now aren't nearly as accepting of criticism from coaches as we were. I'm talking about even the mildest criticism. They're not even receptive to their parents' criticism. Basic coaching is something they consider criticism. I guess it's like that for kids of this era no matter what they do.[5]

Don't let that statement by Charles Barkley be true of your child. Help your child turn criticism into improvement.

When discouraged or upset by criticism, Allen Iverson turned to Magic Johnson for advice:

> The great Magic Johnson counseled a disgruntled and discouraged Iverson who was having a struggling relationship with his '76ers' coach, "I know what a pain in the ass coaches can be," he said. "Don't forget, I played for Pat Riley. He was much tougher than Larry Brown. But I loved it. And I loved him, because that's how he cared about me.[6]

I like Magic's thought: ". . . that's how he cared about me." Teach your young athlete to remember that message.

As a father, you may have times when your child comes home from practice and you will know from his demeanor that he has had a bad practice for one reason or another. It may be that the coach gave him a tongue-lashing during practice. For your son, the tongue-lashing he gets from a coach may be the first time that anyone has ever yelled at him for making a mistake. I mean really yelled at him! It might be the first time anyone has ever been strongly critical of him.

When your son tells you the coach yelled and screamed because he was not hustling, you can help him understand that occasionally he is going to get an earful from his coach. Strive to help him see that the coach's motivation is to help him become a better basketball player. Advise him that the coach has to figure out the best way to motivate him and the coach may feel he can do that best by yelling at him.

You will have to be wise and strong in this because it will always be difficult to see your son put down in any way. Let your child know that you understand his feelings. However, don't be critical of the coach. Be supportive of him and help your child convert the criticism into something that is positive. Ask him how he can do better and how he can make sure the coach doesn't yell at him for the same reason in the future.

If you respond to such situations by saying the coach doesn't know what he's talking about—if you are critical of the coach—then the next time he yells at your youngster to motivate him, your words are going to come back into his mind. Instead of being motivated, your child will feel resentful and uncooperative.

I'm a father. I know the natural parental reaction to a negative situation with a coach is to give the coach a piece of your mind. Restrain yourself.

Most coaches act the way they act because they want an individual to improve or the team to get better. If you undermine the coach for being critical of your son, then you've done a great disservice to your son.

THE COACH MAKES THE RULES AND THE PLAYER FOLLOWS THEM

A coach will have rules that to him or her are vital. A player may disagree with the rules, but he must keep them. Former UCLA Coach John Wooden had a team rule against facial hair for his players. Coach Wooden writes:

> One day Bill Walton [one of UCLA's star players] came to practice after a ten-day break wearing a beard. I asked him, "Bill , have you forgotten something?" He replied, "Coach, if you mean the beard, I think I should be allowed to wear it. It's my right." I asked, "Do you believe that strongly?" He answered, "Yes, I do, Coach. Very much." I looked at him and said politely, "Bill, I have great respect for individuals who stand up for those things in which they believe. I really do. And the team is going to miss you." Bill went to the locker room and shaved the beard off before practice began. There were no hard feelings. I wasn't angry and he wasn't mad. He understood the choice was between his own desires and the good of the team, and Bill was a team player. I think if I had given in to him I would have lost control not only of Bill but of his teammates.[7]

Learning from the coach who many feel was the greatest coach ever is always wise.

NO JUNK FOOD

During my high school playing days, Coach Spencer asked each of us to eliminate junk food from our diets. I sacrificed soda pop, candy bars, and other sugar goodies. I didn't stop eating junk food because I had to stop. I did it because I wanted to stop. I had an intense desire, an inward drive to be the best. I felt that part of becoming the best was doing what my coach asked me to do, not only in the gym, but away from the gym as well.

YOUR IMPACT UPON YOUR SON'S COACHABILITY

These coachability factors are directed at both you and your child. You must help your athlete place these pieces in their proper place in his All-American Puzzle. Without your help he will not have the maturity and wisdom to understand and do what is needed to be coachable.

From what I have observed as I've watched parents at ball games and as I've talked to them about their child's athletic careers, I feel this part of the book may be the hardest part of all for parents to follow. Yet it is such a vital part of your child's All-American Puzzle. If your youngster is coachable it greatly enhances his chances of enjoying a successful athletic experience. And whether or not your child is coachable is to a large degree in your hands. The way that he relates to coaches will be highly influenced by the way that you relate to them.

As surely as the sun will rise in the morning, your child will have some disappointments in sports. When that happens, don't blame the coach. Coaches aren't perfect. There is much to criticize in the best of them. And the worst of them could be the pain of your life. Your job is to make the best of whatever situation or whatever coach comes into your life. If you criticize and belittle the coach in the presence of your child, it will poison his relationship with his coach and will prevent him, during that season, from progressing as he should.

HOPE FOR THE BEST AND MAKE THE BEST OF THE WORST

One of life's sweetest blessings is to have your child come under the influence of an excellent coach. A coach who will make great demands and who will teach accountability. A coach who will influence him to become a better player and a better person. On the other hand, one of your great trials will be to have your son come under the direction of what you feel is an incompetent, insensitive, or unfair coach. Your child may also have to spend a season with a coach who is a ranting and raving wild man. Or worse, he may have a coach who is so nice that there is no discipline on the team, or your son may suffer under the direction of a person who has been assigned to be the coach of the team with very little knowledge about the game. Because your child will have many coaches in his career, he will likely get at least one of each kind. Your job is to help him get the most out of each experience. That can be accomplished by being as positive as you can in each situation.

PREPARE INSTEAD OF COMPLAIN

Over the years, I have heard the following from parents: "My son didn't make the varsity team because the coach had the team picked back when these kids were in eighth grade." "My daughter didn't make the team because the selection of the team is so political." "My son only plays a few minutes a game because the coach doesn't recognize talent." I could go on for a long time rehearsing the many excuses and complaints I have heard about various coaches and the many reasons why a child did not make the team or why he or she doesn't get much playing time.

Of course there will be times when your child is playing on a team when a coach shows favoritism for one reason or another. That is human nature, particularly when the player being favored is the coach's son or daughter. It is also human nature for you to assume that when your athlete does not get a generous amount of opportunity, it is because the coach is showing favoritism. The best way to make favoritism a non-issue in your child's athletic career is to help him become a better player. Then suddenly the favoritism will favor your child. You can then assure the other parents with confidence that one of the coach's best qualities is that he does not show favoritism.

I'm kidding around a little with this touchy subject because there will be times when dealing with a coach requires a good sense of humor. At other times you may even shed some tears for your child because of disappointments caused by coaches. Roll with the punches and remember that in time the rewards will far outweigh the heartaches.

Leave the excuses for someone else. What is wrong with saying, "My son didn't make the team because the other boys are better players than he is," or "My daughter is on the bench because the girls on the floor are more skilled?"

Rather than blame a coach, accept that the real answer to the playing time problem may be that there wasn't enough preparation on your child's part before the season began. Sometimes you might just have to endure a season and make the most of a bad situation. Help your youngster understand by saying, "Next off-season we've got to improve our preparation. We'll work together to develop your skills to the point where you don't have to sit on the bench." This will help your child make it through a tough time. Your best response is to learn from the situation and determine that next year will be different because you and your athlete are going to prepare better during the off-season.

You might say to me, "I know what you say is usually true. However, my son's coach is an idiot. He just doesn't get it." I hear you. There will surely be times when you, as a parent, feel like you know more than your son's coach. And you may. I've certainly felt those emotions towards some of my children's coaches. Maybe even your son will feel that he is more knowledgeable than the coach. I would say that it is irrelevant how much you know about the game or how much your son knows about the game because for a period of time, the coach is the coach. You need to respect that—do as he says—and make the decision to learn what you can from the coach.

I admire people who choose to be coaches. They give a lot of time to help young people. I particularly admire tough coaches. However, I want to make it clear that I am talking about "good people" who are tough coaches. I know, as you do, out there in the world there are some bad people. Occasionally, one of them chooses to be a coach.

If your child's coach turns out to be a bad person and crosses the line from being a tough coach to violating parental trust or to breaking the law in any way, waste no time in distancing yourself and your child from that person.

TEACH ACCOUNTABILITY

One of the pluses of participating in athletics is that it teaches accountability. When your child is out there playing and he makes a mistake, he is immediately held accountable. That might mean that he will be taken out of the game and get to sit on the bench for a while, or even for the rest of the game. That could happen because the coach is making him accountable for his mistakes.

Some parents face the temptation of wanting to bail their child out and not allow him to be accountable. If you are always blaming someone else and never holding your own child accountable, you are doing him a tremendous disservice that will hamper him on and off the court. Pat Summitt, the very successful coach of the women's basketball team at the University of Tennessee, said:

> Accountability is essential to personal growth, as well as team growth. How can you improve if you're never wrong? If you don't admit a mistake and take responsibility for it, you're bound to make the same one again.[8]

TEACH RESPECT

Sports also gives you a wonderful opportunity to teach your child about respect. As you teach him to respect his coach, you are also teaching him to respect parents and to respect other authority figures. If you do the opposite it can have a negative impact upon your child. As he goes out into the work force it will be difficult for him to take criticism from a supervisor if he has not learned respect for authority. He might also be critical of co-workers. One of the greatest gifts you can give your child is to teach him to respect others.

On a related note, negative comments about your child's coach made to your child, or to others when your child is present, might also interfere with the relationship that he could develop with that coach. If you have something negative to say about the coach—his tactics, offensive or defensive scheme, or the players he plays—hold it until the season is over. Then you can sit down and correct anything that you feel like the coach might have erroneously taught your child. But during the season do not do anything that would undermine the coach's effort to help the team win and your child to become a better player.

A COACH CAN MAKE A MIGHTY DIFFERENCE

What I have said thus far may seem a bit negative, as if most coaches are going to be a problem. Not so! Most coaches are vitally interested in their players and they know the values that sports can teach your family member. When you get a coach who makes your child stretch to his limits and beyond, be grateful. This man that your child calls "coach" can be a great influence for good.

As you think back, consider who has been the most influential person in your life. Who has blessed your life and taught you valuable principles? My guess is that for most people, it was a parent; if not, it may have been a school teacher or a coach. What kind of teachers were your parents? Do you feel like they helped you become a better person? How did they do that? What about your coaches and school teachers? How did they help you? In so many cases it seems the ones we look back on most fondly are probably the ones that pushed us the hardest.

I don't think my father really ever fully knew what I went through with Coach Bolus. I didn't say much about it at the time. If I had told my Dad everything I was going through with him, he might have wondered what Coach Bolus' motives were and why he was pushing his team so hard when they were so young. However, it is my hope that he would have picked up the phone, dialed my coach's number, and said, "Thank you. Thank you very much for what you are doing to help my son improve as a basketball player and as a man."

LOOKING BACK WITH GRATITUDE TO MY COACHES

I thank Rick Bolus. He made me work harder than I ever had up to that point in my life.

I thank Mike Hash, my ninth grade coach. He loved the game. He said and did things that gave me confidence. He told me to play to my strengths so I could complement the other four starters—Buck, Willie, Luster, and Gregory—who were like brothers to me. He gave me the freedom to come out of myself and play for the joy of the game.

I thank Jim Spencer, my high school coach. He taught me that the fundamentals of the game were the building blocks of victory. He admired John Wooden and he taught us many of the principles that Coach Wooden taught his players at UCLA. Coach Spencer made me part of a winning tradition and taught me to expect to win and to do what it took to deserve victory.

I thank Frank Arnold, my first college coach. He taught me that as a member of the BYU team I represented far more than just myself. I represented my university, my family, and my church. He taught me to conduct myself with dignity. He also taught me to speak my mind. We often went to lunch together and he would invite me to tell him how I was feeling. He would listen to me and my concerns. Things didn't always have to be his way. One time he told me that he thought I wasn't active enough on the floor—that I could put forth more effort. As we talked I explained that I just was not a "herky-jerky" type of player, but that I always gave everything I had. He understood my feelings, and my effort during games was never again an issue. He decided to focus on what he liked about my game and on what I was able to produce rather than on my style of play. He trusted me by taking the risk of making me a starter for him as a freshman. Because of his trust and encouragement I gained valuable experience early in my college years.

I thank Ladell Andersen, my second college coach. He coached me during my senior year. He allowed me to showcase my abilities. He let me know he would not take me out of the game until my eligibility ran out. Without his belief in me and the freedom he gave me on the court, I would not have made All-American.

And most of all, I thank my father. By watching him interact with others, I was able to learn how to be coachable so that these other men could do their job.

To all my coaches, I offer a heartfelt thanks for providing so many of the pieces that I needed over the years to complete my All-American Puzzle.

Devin Durrant's
All-American Puzzle

PART 4
WORK, WORK, WORK

CONSCRIPT OR VOLUNTEER

Work is the part of the All-American Puzzle that separates the good from the great. The coach can work your son hard enough to make him a good player, but your son is the one who must force himself to work hard enough to become a great player.

The army has two types of soldiers. One is a conscript. A conscript has been drafted and forced by the government to serve. The other is a volunteer. He is there of his own free will. Generally speaking, conscripts do their duty, and volunteers are those who go beyond the call of duty. Truly great athletes are always volunteers, not conscripts.

The following is an account of a boy who was at first a conscript. He then decided on his own to become a volunteer and to do the impossible.

THE FIVE-DOLLAR JOB

Years ago I remember hearing a story of a young boy who was forced into mowing the lawn of an older lady who lived in his town. The account had quite an impact on me because I mowed a lot of lawns growing up and I could relate very well to the boy in the story.

It begins with the boy showing up for the first time to mow the lady's lawn. When he finished the job, she was not satisfied. She made him go over the lawn three additional times before she would allow him to stop working. When he finished for the second time she asked him how much he felt the work was worth that he had done. He suggested fifty cents.

She gave him that amount and then added a dollar and a half. She told him the extra money was payment for the effort he made because of her insistence that he improve his performance.

She then told him to come again the next week and do the same work that he had just done, but next time without her supervision. She told him that if he did as she requested, she would pay him three dollars. They agreed that in the future he would be paid based on the quality of his work. She then made it clear that each week it would be up to him to report to her what he felt his work was worth. She expressed to him that she thought he was probably a three-dollar-job kind of worker. She went on to say that it would be extremely difficult for him to do a four-dollar job and that he would be a fool to even try. As he was about to leave, she added that a five-dollar job would be impossible and he should never even consider that outcome.

He liked the idea of his pay being tied to the quality of his work. For a few weeks, with some good effort, he consistently did a three-dollar job. At first he was happy with that. But gradually he felt he could do better. Then one day as he walked to the woman's house he decided that he would try to do a four-dollar job. He eagerly began, however the summer's sun was hot and the lawn was so big. He grew tired and finally decided that a three-dollar job was good enough.

On his way home he thought of himself as a failure. That

was not a good feeling. Then suddenly a thought came into his mind. He decided that what he really wanted to do was not the four-dollar job, but the five-dollar job. He knew the five-dollar job was impossible for a young boy. However, he knew it was what he had to do. His heart began to pound with excitement. He could hardly sleep for the next several days as he thought about all the work he could do to make the lady's yard beautiful. He was determined to do the impossible—the five-dollar job.

The big day finally arrived. He began early in the morning. He mowed the lawn. Then he raked. Then he mowed the lawn again in the other direction. Then he trimmed the edges. He also trimmed bushes and weeded flower beds. He repeated these tasks again and again until they were done exactly right. He worked to exhaustion and then he worked some more.

At sundown, the young boy, drained of all energy, knocked on the lady's door. She opened the door and looked down at him and asked, "How much do I owe you?" The boy responded, "Five dollars."

She was astonished at his reply and decided to inspect his work. As she walked around the yard, she was amazed at the quality of his work. She agreed that he had done the impossible and she paid him accordingly. As he walked home that evening, he felt joy and satisfaction. He had gone far beyond his best. He had found reserves of energy that he never knew he had. He had reached out beyond where others could command him to go. He had truly done a five-dollar job.

THE BENEFITS OF THE FIVE-DOLLAR JOB

At first this boy was a conscript. He felt forced by the lady to show up for work. Initially, he did as little as possible to get by. She then demanded that he do much more. It was her idea, not his, to do the three-dollar job.

Then he decided to do better on his own. However, his

heart was not yet fully in it. He was still a reluctant volunteer. Thus when he claimed he wanted to do a four-dollar job, he was not really committed to do all that it took.

Finally, the breakthrough came. He had an inward prompting that he wanted to be the best. He wanted to do the impossible. He wanted to do the five-dollar job. That is what it takes. That inward commitment to do all the painful work that it takes to achieve a goal. Now it was himself, not the woman, who was driving him. He was his own coach—a committed volunteer reaching for an ideal.

THE MYTH

In athletics there is a lot of talk about giving 110%. An athlete is not capable of giving more than 100%—his full capability. I believe that rarely do the greatest athletes on the face of the earth give more than 90% of what they are capable of giving. I also believe that most young athletes give effort in the 30% to 50% range. Over time and with good instruction they learn to increase their effort. They learn they can give more than their self-imposed limits would allow. Lance Armstrong shares this about exceeding his own limits:

> Johan knew me more by reputation than anything else: a huge talent who didn't get everything out of himself. Every once in a while, I'd deliver a big ride: when I was 21, I had come out of nowhere to win the Worlds, and then a stage of the Tour de France. But mostly I cruised for months at a time, performing decently but not exceptionally, just barely meeting the definition of "professional".
>
> Back then, I thought I was doing all that I could do. After the cancer, I realized I'd been operating at about half of my abilities. The truth was that I'd never trained as hard as I could, never focused as much as I could.[1]

Lance Armstrong was working at 50% of his abilities, and at that level he was still able to win the Worlds. Over time things changed for him and he learned, as well as anyone ever has, how to go beyond his own limits.

GET OUT OF YOUR COMFORT ZONE

When I met Rick Bolus I was probably exerting myself at about 40% of what I was capable of when I competed. As a young boy I thought I had learned how to work from playing baseball and football and helping around the house and in the yard. But when I played under Coach Bolus, everything changed. He forced me to realize what hard work really was. Day after day I was pushed beyond my comfort zone, from my 40% effort to his 70% demands and higher. Without Coach Bolus, I would have stayed within my lower limits. He wouldn't allow that. Coach Bolus demanded that we go beyond those limits every day.

Those who truly could become All-Americans probably spend most of their time at 70% to 90% of what they are capable of doing. So often we set limits on ourselves—how fast we are able to sprint, how far we are able to run, how high we are able to jump.

So it is critical to have someone there, like a hard-driving coach, who figures out ways to motivate us, to get us beyond what we think our limits are. Once we understand how to exceed our personal limits, then we are prepared to coach ourselves and approach our full capacity.

One of my favorite forms of entertainment is witnessing an athlete who is able to reach up close to and sometimes touch 100% of his capabilities. These magical moments are treasures that can inspire your children and mine to reach beyond the comfort zone that they reside in now and reach for the so-called impossible five-dollar job—100% of their capacity.

FIND A DEMANDING COACH

Every All-American can astound you with stories of how hard he worked to get there. He might say, "You think you have it hard . . ." Then he will tell a horror story about what a coach demanded that he do. Here is such a story about a Christmas Day practice told by Pat Conroy, a member of the Citadel University basketball team:

> Practice began promptly at 1600 hours and it was a killer. Coach Thompson kept yelling that he was going to sweat the Christmas turkey out of us. . . . The Christmas practices were a nightmare, a plebe system, one more boot camp run by a sadist who drove us like dogs until we dropped from exhaustion and dry heaves. Since the campus was closed down, there were no time constraints on Mel. And the sessions could be as long as he wanted them to be. . . . The Christmas Day practice lasted three and a half hours. One of us had to puke before he would stop. . . . We joked about having a designated puker. After that, we quit joking about anything.[2]

That's pretty tough stuff. But even so, hearing that story other athletes would say, "If you think that is tough, listen to this." A story of a hard-driving coach will then be told with a lot of emotion. Your young athlete might already have his own stories to tell of times when he was pushed to his limits. If not, I hope that he soon will.

When your son is around the age of 14, try to find a coach for him who is tough and demanding. A coach who treats him like a conscript. A coach who will force him to work harder than he has ever worked before. A coach who will insist that your son go beyond the limits that he thinks he can go. The coach can treat him like a conscript because the coach has the keys to something your young athlete wants. The coach is the one who can allow him to be on the team, to get playing time, and to be a starter. Your son may hate the coach for forcing him to work, but your son will do it because he wants to succeed.

Part of your role as a parent is to open doors for your sons and daughters. Open the door to good coaches. Do your homework and see if there is a coach out there who will stretch your child. One of the saddest things I see is when that type of coach is out there and he is doing just that—he is pushing a child—and the parents take offense. They want to intercede and rescue their child so they step in and demand that a tough coach lighten up. I think in reality they are harming their child who may have the potential to be a fine athlete.

"WE COULDN'T HELP BUT GET BETTER"

A future All-American has to learn to work. Hopefully, the value of hard work will become clear for the young athlete sooner rather than later. The only way to improve as an athlete is to work. A basketball player on his way to stardom can't sit and spin a basketball on his finger and wish his way to stardom. He has to get up and go to work each day to improve. It's that way in every sport and in every pursuit of excellence.

Baseball great Dale Murphy of the Atlanta Braves worked so hard as a young man at baseball with his friends that, in his words, "we couldn't help but get better." He wrote:

> . . . in the summers, all we did was play baseball. I became very dedicated. I'd drill holes in my bats, fill them will lead, and practice swinging them by the hour in the basement.

Dale also worked at a summer baseball day camp with his friends. He continued:

> We practiced with our Legion team for two hours every morning, followed by the day camp. It was the only

job I ever had, and I worked there for three hours a day.
Then we went home to rest for a couple of hours before
batting practice and a Legion game. We'd do that almost
every day. . . . We played so much baseball we couldn't
help but get better.[3]

The seeds that were planted during these summers of hard
work later grew into back-to-back National League MVP
awards for Dale Murphy.

THE HARDEST PART IS TO START

Discuss with your child your understanding of how hard
it is to work out as often as is necessary to become an All-
American. Encourage him continually to keep at it.

Even if your child does well at being his own coach and even
if he loves the game, there will still be times when he will dread
a workout. Such dread causes him to sit and think, "Man! I hate
working out. It's so hard. At times I feel like I'm about to die."
He doesn't dread the entire workout, just the physically taxing
part. Thinking about that part makes him look for excuses to
skip the day's workout.

The hardest part is getting over the mental barrier and
getting the workout clothes on and getting to the gym. Once
there and warmed up, the love of the game usually takes over.

Of course it is up to him. You can't force your child, but you
can talk to him about it. Let him know you understand. Praise
him when you know he is working hard. My dad was an expert
in this area. He always had an encouraging word for me.

Occasionally, you might even want to join your son in
a workout or do some other kind of fun physical activity.
Van't Hof, coach of tennis star Lindsay Davenport, energized
her with some creative workouts, as the following example
shows:

Van't Hof sized Davenport up immediately: her strokes were immaculate, her technique flawless, her hands deceptively quick. But her footwork and fitness were a disaster. Not only was Davenport glacially slow on the court but she hated exercising. Van't Hof set about making training tolerable, if not outright enjoyable, by varying the drills and doing them with Davenport. One day they'd throw a football and run fly patterns on the beach, the next day they'd climb stairs, the next day they'd play basketball. "If someone tells me to go to the gym, I'm like, 'yeah, whatever,' and I'll drive home," says Davenport. "But when you have a coach work out with you it's energizing."[1]

GREEN, YELLOW, AND RED WORK

Discuss with your son the idea of breaking up workouts into green, yellow, or red work.

Green work is the enjoyable work, such as a pickup game. We all love to do the green work.

Yellow work is done when an athlete comes to the gym and finds there is no game. He or she stays and has a vigorous workout that takes the same energy a game would have taken.

Red work is work like lifting weights with so many repetitions that the body cries out to stop or doing a series of wind sprints until the lungs burn. Don't put red work off until later or it may not get done. Teach your athlete to say, "I'll do the hard work first. Then, I'll take care of the more enjoyable parts of my workout such as shooting and playing in pickup games." If there is no game to be found, the "red workers" compete with themselves in shooting contests, working at game speed as much as possible. They find a game and give it their all on offense and defense. They work on their weaknesses. Then they run home and eat nutritious food and get to bed at a reasonable hour. Competing with yourself can make red work so exciting and fulfilling that it becomes green work—or at least yellow work.

Help your future All-American understand the following:

1. Unmotivated athletes will do the green work, at least until they get a bit weary of doing it.
2. Semi-motivated athletes will do the green work faithfully, will do quite well at doing the yellow work, and will even dabble with the red work.
3. The motivated athletes—those who want to do a five-dollar job—are those who hunger and thirst to become an All-American. These athletes revel in doing the green and yellow, but will religiously do the red work.

DO THE RED WORK

As a young professional basketball player, Kobe Bryant knew the importance of doing the "red work." He followed a very tough workout regimen:

> As much as he loved basketball, and as talented as he was, he also knew he would have to become bigger and stronger to compete successfully against the grown men he was facing in the NBA. His rookie year had taught him that much. So during the spring and summer of 1997, Kobe worked harder than he had ever worked in his life. Under the supervision of a personal trainer, Kobe embraced a world-class fitness regimen that would leave most athletes begging for mercy. Six days a week he would drive to a local track and run a series of gut-busting wind sprints. And that was just for a warm-up. Next he would travel to Gold's Gym for a few hours of weight training, followed by two hours of solitary work on his jump shot. Finally, late in the afternoon, he would head over to UCLA to play pickup ball against the best college and professional players in the Los Angeles area.

Typically, he worked out for seven or eight hours a day. One day a week, at his trainer's insistence, he rested so that his body could recover.[5]

Becoming a red worker will cause some to call your son a fanatic and they may question his priorities. That's all right. There is a lot of time in a day. Your son will still have time for non-athletic events and for studies. Tell him to just be sure that he gets the red work done first, then the yellow, and then the green.

WORKING HARDER THAN A FUTURE OPPONENT

If a future opponent works harder than your child, when they meet on the court, chances are he will beat your boy. I remember well some of the opponents that I feared might be working harder than I was as I grew up. In junior high, it was Jerry Eaves from Ballard. In high school, it was first Danny Vranes from Skyline and later Craig Hammer of Murray. In college, it was Pace Mannion from the University of Utah and Fred Reynolds from UTEP. I'd think about these guys all summer as I worked on my own.

I also thought about that imaginary player who might be working even harder than I was. I didn't know his identity yet but I figured somewhere down the road we would meet each other on the court, and I wanted to be ready.

Lance Armstrong prepared himself to compete against future opponents by outworking them. He said:

> I give everything I've got. My performances were the result of hard work; of the fact that I had trained and been on the bike when no one else was riding, in the off-season and in all weather. I'd ridden the Alps in the snow. And I didn't see any other riders there.[6]

Lance went on to explain the confidence that comes from knowing that you have done more than your opponent to prepare for competition:

> Nobody could give that kind of confidence to an athlete, except himself. It couldn't be faked, or called up at the last minute. You got it from everything you did leading up to the competition, so that on the day of the race itself, you looked around at all the other strong riders beside you, and said, "I'm ready. I've done more than they have. Bring it on."[7]

My oldest daughter, Emily, was an excellent high school basketball player. One day she and I were driving to the mall. We stopped at a red traffic signal and waited for it to turn green. Suddenly, crossing in front of us, was Danielle Cheesman. She was running along the street. There was no other traffic on the road, so when the light changed we both sat there and watched this girl run. She had been named Honorable Mention All-American as a high school junior (after her senior year she was named First Team All-American). We watched as she disappeared into a local fitness center. We both knew that her home was some two miles away.

Danielle was to Emily what Pace Mannion was to me. Danielle played for Mountain View High School where she led them to multiple state championships and the ESPN number one ranking in the country for the 2000-01 season. I didn't drive on because I wanted Emily to see what she was up against. I didn't say anything. I didn't need to. Emily knew what she needed to do.

A few months later when Emily and her Timpanogos teammates were set to play against Mountain View, Emily was beside herself with a desire to win that game. She could hardly sleep. She had never in her life wanted anything so badly as to beat Danielle Cheesman and the talented Mountain View girls who were coached by Dave Houle, the most successful high school coach ever with over 66 state championships to his credit.

However, all the desire and all the wishing could not make it so. Emily had not converted her wishing into action months earlier when she saw Danielle running to work out at the fitness center. Danielle recently completed four very successful years of basketball at BYU.

MUSCLE CRAMPS

I remember a game we played against LaSalle University while I was at BYU. It was a hard-fought game from the beginning. We would get ahead and then their star, Michael Brooks, would hit a couple of difficult shots and the score would be even again. By the end of the night, Michael would set a Marriott Center record by scoring 51 points.

I was a freshman at the time. As the clock wound down I was grateful it would soon be over. I had given my all and I was dead tired.

Finally, the game clock ran out. I have never before been so totally exhausted. However, sadly, we had not won. The score was tied and we now faced overtime. I struggled to find energy as we waited to take the floor again. New strength entered my body. Again I gave it my all. The clock was winding down and the score went back and forth—the lead was ours and then theirs.

Again the clock expired, but again the score was tied. I headed for the bench and sat down. In what seemed like a brief moment, the referee called us back to center court. I was fatigued as never before. They got the tip and raced down the floor. I was with my man. I could not let him score. My assignment was greater than my fatigue. Up and down the court I ran. I jumped. I passed. I shot. I defended. Finally the clock wound down and again the score was even.

In the third overtime I was more determined than ever that we would not lose. I had too much invested in this game to lose it. I jumped to get a rebound that I knew we had to get to survive. I got the ball but as I landed my legs collapsed with the pain of muscle cramps. I passed the ball off and pain shot up my legs. I tried to run as the cramps tightened. There was no way to call time out and I had to continue. I did my best to hobble up the court. Again the clock went to 0:00. This time we were up by two precious points. The battle was over and I had survived. That victory was a sweet paycheck for all the hard work my teammates and I had put in as we conditioned and prepared for that season.

Hard work precedes the athlete's paycheck—victory.

DESERVE SUCCESS

To be confident, you have to know within yourself that you have done the things that you need to do to be good. Coach Rick Pitino makes it clear that you have to deserve success in order to gain the confidence that precedes success. He forcefully teaches:

> Self-esteem is directly linked to deserving success. If you have established a great work ethic and have begun the discipline that is inherent with that, you will automatically begin to feel better about yourself. It's all interrelated. You must deserve victory to feel good about yourself.[8]

Pitino's words—self-esteem, great work ethic, discipline, victory—are the ingredients in the recipe for excellence.

KEEP YOUR EYE ON THE PRIZE

Help your youngster to see a vision of himself being named a starter and of his team winning the championship. Such a dream will help him through the pain of doing red work. It will help him work harder to achieve excellence. It will help him do what he needs to do to feel confident. It will give him the determination to do what it takes to outwork his opponent. Pitino went on to say:

> . . . You must keep your eye on the prize. You must keep telling yourself that the end is going to be worth the means. We see this in sports all the time, the amazing outpouring of emotion after a team wins a championship. Part of that is the thrill of victory, obviously. But it's more than that too. It's the realization of how hard they worked to get there, all the long hours, all the hard work, all the sweat. That's what you think about when you win a championship: how hard you have worked for it.[9]

BE RESPONSIBLE

I feel strongly that dedication to sports is a great vehicle in which to have a most exciting ride and in which to learn the lasting qualities of being a responsible person. Teach your child the virtue of being responsible for his own life. Driving yourself physically is part of it, but not all. Hard work is also being responsible. It is being there when you would rather be somewhere else. It is staying with a job until it is completely done, the tools are put away, and the shop is clean. Hard work is as much mental as it is physical. Mental strength allows an athlete to make grueling physical effort.

DON'T MAKE YOUR SON
A CONSCRIPT

Don't make a conscript out of your son where you are the master and he is the servant. That situation is not for you. It is for the coach. It is all right if your child hates the coach. But it is not all right if he despises you. Although you can teach and encourage, you cannot compel your youngster to be a hard worker. It is only when your athlete begins to do things of his own free will that hard work will become a personal habit. It is only when your son does things that he feels an inward drive to do, that he will truly become a hard worker.

THE PAPER ROUTE

Farms demand hard work. Unfortunately, the opportunity to have our children work a long day on a farm is not available to most of us. Nevertheless, children need opportunities to work. One simple work alternative is a paper route.

A story is told of a young paperboy who had an early morning paper route. He worked at this job all summer and fall. Then came winter. On a blizzardy morning he folded his papers and set out. It was cold and the snowdrifts were deep. He had to push his bike more than he rode it. His route was on the outskirts of town and there was some distance between houses. But he had to keep going. There was no choice. After a bitter struggle with the elements, he finally delivered the last paper and made the long journey home. He was nearly frozen and totally exhausted.

Later that day, he announced to his father that he had decided to give up the paper route. His father's reply changed his life. The older, wiser man said, "That's okay with me. But you can't quit now. Wait until summer and then you can quit."

It is no wonder that the young paper boy grew up and became a successful businessman through his hard work and industry. The only time he ever quit a job was when it was going well and he wanted to move on to a greater challenge. Symbolically speaking, he never quit in the winter. If your child asks you, "Can I quit the team?" You might reply, "You can quit when you have gone through all the pre-season practices and when you have worked yourself into excellent shape. Then you can quit."

Start teaching your child to work when he is young but

don't expect an elementary-age child to do really hard work. However, do give him tasks to complete and be firm in seeing that he completes them. Insist that he be responsible in caring for things and being where he is supposed to be when he is supposed to be there. It is out of this kind of soil that the seeds of hard work will grow.

Try to develop habits in your son that will make him a hard worker. You can push him a bit, but at a certain point it becomes very difficult for you to be the one who pushes him beyond his limits. If your son's desire to work hard in athletics, of his own free will, does not manifest itself, then there is nothing you can do to change that. On the other hand, if your son does decide, on his own, to give his all to a sport, then there will be no way for you or anyone else to stop him. It is this decision to do it on his own that will give a young athlete a vital part of his All-American Puzzle.

If he does not make the decision to work hard as an athlete, then back off, abandon any idea of force, and enjoy your child for what he does decide to pursue.

TWO GOALS FOR OUR YOUNG ATHLETES

Let me suggest two goals for your children and mine. First and foremost, let's help our children fulfill their full potential as human beings. Second, let's help them reach the highest level they can as athletes or in whatever pursuit they choose. The process for the accomplishment of these two goals is not the same.

As a parent, you will have the role of molding a child into a responsible adult. In this role, if he doesn't do his homework, he needs to be taught that in your family that is not acceptable— he has to do schoolwork. If your child lies, you need to let him know that dishonesty is not an option in his family—he has to be honest. You may want to give your son some guidance on his appearance and so on. Your role in this part of your child's life does not end in junior high, or high school, or even college. For some parents, it never ends.

GET A HAIRCUT

A couple of months ago I visited with my mom and dad. Each of them commented on the fact that my hair was getting a little long. Neither one of them said directly to me, "Your hair is too long. You need a haircut." But each, in their own way, hinted to me that it was time to get a haircut. That was a nice experience because it helped me remember once again how much my parents love me and how they still want me to look like a responsible adult.

They no longer have any concerns about me becoming a successful athlete, however. Their concern with that ended years ago. Today their concern is for me as a husband and as the father of six of their grandchildren. They want me to be honorable and to have integrity and to look the part.

It is one thing to insist that your child practice his sport. It is another when you insist that he does his homework. When you insist that he perform his duties in his school and family life, you can set certain punishments if he does not comply. But imposing any punishment for a lack of effort in sports will dampen the love your child needs to have for the game. With certain aspects of his character education, your youngster will often do things because he has to. In his sports life, your son should only be involved because he wants to be. I don't mean that you won't encourage him in sports, but there should be no need to force him.

As a parent, you will have great influence in your son's early years of athletics. You can teach him basic skills, help him feel confident, entice him to have a love of the game, but as he gets older, your influence in his athletic career will diminish. While you will always use your influence to raise a responsible adult, the time will come when you must step back for your child to pursue his All-American dream on his own.

STEP BACK

As your child gets older and starts into junior high and high school, if he hasn't begun to capture the idea of being his own coach and taking responsibility for his athletic progress, then there is not a lot you can do to change that. Hopefully, at about the age when you need to step back you will be fortunate enough to find another significant adult, probably a coach or a teacher, who will step forward—someone else outside the family who can help push your child.

Placing the pieces in the work, work, work part of your child's All-American Puzzle might be the most difficult part of the puzzle for him. If he is able to complete this difficult part he will find great joy in sports. Your son will also find success and satisfaction in the ventures he pursues outside of athletics because he will have learned an essential element of success in life—how to work, work, work.

DEVIN DURRANT'S
ALL-AMERICAN PUZZLE

PART 5
RODEO TOUGH

COMPETITIVE AND TOUGH

My boys and I play a simple game called, "Who's The Toughest?" The game is played with two people. Both participants place both hands on a basketball and get the best grip that they can. The signal is given to begin and each player tries to rip the ball away from the other. It's a fun game that teaches the importance of strong hands in the game of basketball and the proper technique to rip the ball out of an opponent's hands.

How would you respond if I asked you to name the sport which is made up of the toughest athletes? The toughest athletes mentally and the toughest athletes physically? I have thought about this a great deal. I am not sure of the answer. I have always had great respect for the mental toughness of marathon runners and long-distance swimmers. Gymnasts amaze me with their long hours of practice and incredible feats of body control and strength. Because of Muhammad Ali, I have always admired the sport of boxing. Golf also requires a great deal of mental toughness. There may be nothing mentally tougher than the back nine of a golf major. What about driving a race car at over 200 miles an hour for 500 miles? Imagine the mental and physical strain that would cause. I could go on and on about the mental or physical toughness required to participate in this or that sport. However, after watching the cowboys ride the big bulls at the rodeo, I think they may just be the toughest athletes around. They ride an animal that weighs many times more than they do and they have no control over that animal. Every bull ride carries the risk of broken bones from the face down to the feet. Bull riders are "rodeo tough."

Toughness and a competitive spirit go together like mashed potatoes and gravy. You can't enjoy one without the other. It is a tremendous advantage for a coach to have a tough competitor on a team. You just know that when the chips are down, he will come through. The fans of his team love such a player and the fans of the other team loathe him.

I played with—and watched closely—two such athletes, Danny Ainge and Steve Young. Both were incredible refuse-to-lose athletes who enjoyed remarkable professional careers. As pros, both were part of championship teams—Danny with the Boston Celtics and Steve with the San Francisco 49ers. But it was what I saw in each of them while they were playing in college that convinced me that they would excel throughout their lives both on and off the field of competition.

Late in a football game between BYU and Utah State University with the game in doubt, Steve was carrying the ball toward his goal line. He got hit by several USU players but he refused to go down. He continue to fight with every ounce of energy to cross the goal line and score the winning touchdown. Somehow he made it through what seemed to be a concrete wall of USU players. He was not going to let his team lose when he was the quarterback. He showed tremendous heart throughout his professional career, but I never saw him display his amazing will to win as I did that day on that scoring run against his in-state rival Utah State.

I played basketball with Danny Ainge during my first two years at BYU. Near the end of my freshman year, we were playing against the San Diego State Aztecs. The conference championship was on the line. With just under two minutes to play, we were down by seven points. I had fouled out and from my seat on the bench, I watched Danny turn a seven-point deficit into a victory in under two minutes. He was incredible that night as he made the defensive plays and big baskets to turn a sure defeat into a conference championship victory. I knew then that Danny Ainge epitomized the term "winner." He loved to compete and, for Danny, losing was not an option.

I get excited writing about athletes like Steve Young and Danny Ainge and thinking about the meaning of "rodeo tough." To me that term means being intensely competitive by being mentally and physically strong. I expect that someday Steve will be in the White House and Danny will be the commissioner of the NBA.

YOU KNOW IT WHEN YOU SEE IT

When I attended one of my son Ryan's flag football games last year, I immediately spotted a boy on his team who had an air of toughness. He was all over the place, tearing the flags from the opponents while playing defense, and darting and racing to keep them from getting his flag while playing offense. He was a talented young man on the field, but what added to his effectiveness was his attitude—his toughness and his competitiveness. After the game, I asked Ryan to tell me about his teammate. He replied, "Oh, yeah. Charlie. He's really tough! His dad rides in rodeos and so does he." That was all I needed to hear.

How would we describe Michael Jordan? "He is quick. He is fast. He can jump. He is smart." We could go on. However, I believe he is best described by these words—mentally tough and relentlessly competitive. A former teammate witnessed Michael's competitiveness every day and said this of him:

> He and I practiced every day together and he always had to win. If it was a game of h-o-r-s-e and you beat him, you would have to play another game until he won. . . . You didn't go home until he had won.[1]

Michael once said:

> Every time I step on the court, if you're against me, you're trying to take something from me. I don't want the other team to win. I just do not want them to win.[2]

COACHES CRAVE THE MENTALLY TOUGH PLAYERS

Dean Smith, the fabled coach of the very successful North Carolina Tar Heels, tried to recruit mentally tough players:

> Of course, we were right to want Phil [Ford] as badly as we did, but not just for the obvious reasons. Recruiting couldn't tell you what was inside of a young man's heart, whether he had the drive to match his physical talent. Phil had as much as anyone I've seen. Every year on the first day of practice we made the players do a timed mile run to check their conditioning. When Phil was a freshman, we went over to this old cinder track at a prep school nearby. Phil came down the line running just slightly behind his time. He accelerated and then accelerated again. As he raced toward the finish line, he suddenly dived, headfirst. He launched himself across the line and hit the cinder track in full roll. When he stood up, he was raw and bleeding. But he had made his time. I couldn't believe it. I

thought, this guy wants it. I didn't bother to go over and see about Phil, although our trainer Marc Davis did. I just hit the button on my stopwatch and turned to my assistants, Bill Guthridge and Eddie Fogler, who were open-mouthed. "We've got ourselves a player," I said.

That same toughness surfaced when Phil was playing against Clemson in the 1976 ACC tourney. An elbow accidentally hit Phil in the mouth, knocking his front tooth out. He picked up the tooth, took a pass and dribbled over to our bench with the clock running, and handed the tooth to our trainer, John Lacey. He now has a false tooth there.[3]

I can see in my mind Phil Ford lunging to make the time and later handing his tooth to the trainer during a game. I admire effort and toughness like that. Your boy might have to pass through similar experiences at times when he competes. You can help him to have the drive that will magnify his talent.

THE TOUGHNESS TEST

Is your son mentally tough? Is he competitive? Ask him the following questions. They will give you a good idea about his competitive spirit and mental toughness. Ask yourself the same questions:

- Do you want to be involved in the final play of a game that will determine if your team wins or loses?
- Do you play best in front of a hostile crowd?
- Would you prefer to play the best team in the league every game instead of the weaker teams?
- Do the taunts of an opponent distract you?
- Do you have the confidence to go against the coach's direction when you see an opportunity to make a game-winning play?
- Do you enjoy the challenge of being an underdog?
- Do you love to defend the other team's best player?

+ Do you love to play in the big games?
+ Do you love the challenge of bettering yourself and outdoing your opponent?
+ Do you take the coach's criticism without crumbling?
+ Can you make a mistake and get right back into the competition with increased desire?
+ Near the end of a tight game, do you run to or away from the ball?
+ Do you dislike losing so much that your stomach aches after a loss?
+ Do you give everything you have and more to get a win?
+ Do you do all you can to get playing time and to make the most of it when you get it?
+ Do you hurt when your team loses even if you played a great individual game?

How did your future All-American do? Did he answer "yes" to all these questions? What about you?

To become an All-American, your son will need to be able to respond in the affirmative to these questions. He will need to learn to be "rodeo tough" and fiercely competitive.

To athletes everywhere, Pat Summitt, who is without a doubt "rodeo tough" says:

> Ask yourself, are you a competitor? Are you selecting weak competition, or strong? Are you settling for less, or reaching for more? When you compete, refuse to limit yourself. Elect to overachieve instead of underachieve. Believe me, you will surprise yourself.[4]

THE INSULT

I gave a talk once at a junior high during their career day. I had been asked to talk about what it took to play in the NBA, and most of my talk centered around the importance of getting a good education because the chance of ever playing in the NBA is extremely remote. I told the kids that I only knew of two people from Utah County who had ever played in the NBA. I emphasized education again and told them I didn't think any of them would ever play in the NBA.

My daughter was in this class, and after my speech one boy told her that I had insulted him because he was convinced that he would make it to the NBA. I was impressed to learn of the feeling of this young man. It takes that kind of competitive attitude to gain the mental toughness necessary to make it to the top.

I recently watched this young man play in the state tournament. Though only a sophomore, he hit a crucial, pressure-packed three-pointer late in the fourth quarter to help his team—Provo High School—win the state championship. He is on his way.

Your child can't be content to be in the middle of the pack. He or she must have the drive to make it to the front. With such drive, mental toughness will follow as surely as the night follows the day.

HUSTLE EVEN WHEN YOU ARE TIRED

Point out to your future All-American that now is the time to hustle. Not next week. Not during the first game. Not in the tournament. Not just in the fourth quarter. Now. Every day, every personal and team practice, every minute of every game. Your son's competitive behavior may cause his teammates to become irritated with him at times. He may be told to slow down. To take it easy. Encourage your son to refuse to take it easy. Teach him to be like the great ones. Teach him to push himself to improve every chance he gets.

Encourage your child, when he is coaching himself, to hustle when he feels he is just too tired to hustle, to pretend he has to get the rebound, or shut down the person he is guarding, or the game will be lost. The adrenaline will flow as he imagines that he must make a key play to seal a victory.

LOVE TO DEFEND

Playing offense is fun. Offense will get your son's name in the newspaper. But for those who enjoy watching a competitor, they look for those who love to shut down their man. The knowledgeable fan and the wise coach love to see a hard-nosed, fiercely competitive, "rodeo tough" defender. There is always room on the starting five for a tough defender. Some nights the offense won't be there—the shots just won't fall—but there is never a game in which your son can't do his job on the defensive end. The following was said about Michael Jordan:

> On certain nights your offensive skills desert you but because defense is a product of hard work, it will always be there. Jordan's teammates could see that idea begin to take hold in his second year, as it became increasingly obvious that on certain nights he was more interested in his defense than his offense and was concentrating on shutting down his man.[5]

Be like Mike and concentrate on shutting down your opponent.

DEAL WITH PAIN

Help your child understand that sometimes athletes hurt a little when they are playing. Sometimes they hurt a lot.

Pain is a sifter that separates the mentally tough from those who are not. The mentally tough athlete is able to play through pain and recognize that it is part of athletics. Those who lack mental toughness will take the opportunity to remove themselves from competition because of pain.

Sometimes athletes are injured and simply can't play. But at other times they are just sore and they could play if they had the necessary mental toughness. A future All-American must be able to tell the difference. He should not play if it might cause further injury to himself. But if there is no risk of further injury, there is no need to shy away from pain. Most high-level athletes just learn to live with varying degrees of pain because it always seems to be with them.

At the beginning of my senior year in high school, I suffered from muscle spasms in my back. At times the pain was so intense it was difficult to walk. After consulting with medical professionals, I learned that with a few weeks of rest and treatment I would be fine. I told my doctor that I wasn't interested in resting at that point because my season had started. He then said that if I wore a back brace and had daily treatment, I could probably play. It was at that point that Marv Roberson and I got to know each other.

Marv was a physical therapist who weighed approximately 300 pounds. Each day before practice I would pay Marv a visit. He would warm up my back and then he would begin to massage the tight muscles in my lower back. First he would massage my back with his hands. Then he would place his elbow on the back muscles. He wouldn't apply much pressure at first but after a time he would increase the pressure. I don't think I can adequately describe the pain I felt as this large man proceeded to try to get my spasmed muscles to relax.

Marv would work on me for 30 to 45 minutes a day. By the time my "torture sessions" were complete, the muscles in my back would relax. I would then go to practice or to a game, strap on my back brace, and compete with my teammates. Marv made it so I could play. Sure I felt pain but I wasn't at risk of further injury. I'll always be grateful to "Marvelous" Marv Roberson for keeping me on the court at a very important time in my life.

Larry Bird played in pain most of his professional career.

His philosophy on playing through pain is revealed in this quote:

> I played some of my best games when I had a muscle pull or I was sick. You come in that night figuring you can't feel any worse, and when you finally get out there and run around a little bit, you tend to forget about what was bothering you.[6]

Pain and athletics seem to go hand in hand. I don't believe there is a successful athlete out there who couldn't tell you a variety of stories about the pain he has had to deal with along the way. Maybe that is why people in the sports medicine field have more than enough work to do. Encourage your child to develop mental toughness to help him deal with the inevitable physical pain of athletics. Mental toughness will also help him deal with the sting of criticism.

DON'T CRUMBLE WHEN CRITICIZED

Hopefully, your son will have a coach who will criticize him when deserved. It will hurt. But that is okay. Teach your son to not ignore what a coach says, but to do something about it. Encourage him to show the coach by his actions that he got the message. Many coaches use criticism to motivate their athletes. Prepare your son for it.

If your son can develop mental toughness, it will have a long-lasting, positive impact on him. After I stopped playing basketball professionally, I worked for a large computer software company. The executive vice-president was a man named Pete Peterson. I remember Pete making the comment that he was always looking to hire athletes because he knew athletes had been put in situations where they had been criticized and that they had developed the mental toughness to bounce back and continue to do their job. This same type of mental toughness often appears in members of a marching band, cheerleading squad, or a dance team—as well as other groups that demand excellence from their members.

An athlete cannot afford to crumble when criticized. He has to be like a rock. He can be soft in other areas of his life, but he has to be strong when the pressure is on.

A mentally tough athlete's desire to win causes him to perform best when he is under the intense pressure of fierce competition and when the game is on the line. He has the mental power to shut out distractions and to concentrate on what needs to be done to win. My sons and I call this the PUP Principle for "Perform Under Pressure."

CRAVE A HOSTILE ENVIRONMENT AND AN AGGRESSIVE OPPONENT

A mentally tough competitor usually plays his best games on the road. He enjoys the hostile environment. He isn't bothered by the wrath of the opposition when he gets into an opponent's gym filled with students from the opposing school.

It gets even more intense in college. While at BYU, I was able to play in some wonderfully hostile environments. Two places immediately come to mind—Laramie, Wyoming, and Albuquerque, New Mexico.

The fans at both places had a lot of emotion and energy. They would yell and scream from the minute we walked on to the floor 30 minutes before the game until we walked off. They had something to say about each of us, our parents, our grandparents, and on down the line.

I loved Albuquerque because one of the best feelings in sports is to have a gym of 18,000 people on their feet yelling and screaming for their team and against yours. In the midst of the noise, you make a basket and get fouled.

While you walk to the foul line, the fans quiet down and they take their seats. It is an even better feeling to quiet your opponent's gym through your play than to have your home crowd stand and cheer—although that feels pretty good, too. When your son is mentally tough, he will enjoy going into tough situations and coming out as the victor.

DEALING WITH OVERLY AGGRESSIVE OPPONENTS

As a young man, I spent a lot of time watching Julius Erving play. He was the best in my eyes. Many years ago when Julius Erving played for the New York Nets, he would come to Freedom Hall in Louisville, Kentucky. The Kentucky Colonels, in the old ABA, would send in a guy named Wendell Ladner, whose main job was to try to get Erving to lose his cool. I watched many a night where Erving would have his way on the court with Ladner. Erving had to be mentally tough each night so that he did not allow his opponent to get under his skin and throw his game off.

Another prime example of a player who had the inner toughness to deal with an overly aggressive opponent was Michael Jordan. His coach, Phil Jackson, loved the idea of a player being a "peaceful warrior." He saw that oxymoron fulfilled in Jordan. Jackson said:

> In my mind, Michael is the epitome of the peaceful warrior. Day in and day out, he has endured more punishment than any other player in the league, but he rarely shows any sign of anger. Once he was upended by Detroit's front line on his way to the basket and brutally slammed to the floor. It was a malicious hit that could have caused serious damage, and I expected Michael to be fuming. But he wasn't. During the timeout that followed, I asked him if he was feeling frustrated. "No," he replied with a shrug, "I know they're going to do that when I'm in there."[7]

Michael was mentally tough enough to do what he had to do no matter what others did to oppose him.

I am a Utah Jazz fan. Today, my favorite Jazz player is Andre Kirilenko. I love the way he gives his all every night to help his team. He amazes me with the plays he is able to make, particularly on the defensive end of the court. He impresses me as a player with tremendous mental toughness. Mentally tough players do not complain about the referees or the opposing fans or the other players or the coach or teammates. They just go out and give their best effort every game to help their team win in any way they can. To me, that is Kirilenko.

As I write about the epitome of the mentally tough player, another Jazz great comes to mind—John Stockton. I don't know of too many players who gave the kind of effort that Stockton did every time he stepped on the floor. He was tough and he feared no one.

THRIVE ON PRESSURE

As someone said, "If you can't take the heat, get out of the kitchen." A mentally tough athlete can not only take the heat, he enjoys it. I would say to young athletes, "If you enjoy the heat, come join me in the kitchen."

Near the end of my senior season at BYU we were playing in Laramie, against the University of Wyoming in a game that would determine the conference championship. Near the end of the game, I drove to the basket and was fouled. My team was down by one point with only three seconds to play. I knew I would have a one and one to win the game. I started to walk toward the foul line. I had rehearsed opportunities like this in my mind hundreds of times. I knew I would make both shots and we would win the conference championship—my fourth in four years. I couldn't have scripted it any better.

Out of the corner of my eye I saw one of the officials waving his arms. As I stood ready to shoot, he hurried to me and said, "You've got the ball out on the side." I didn't understand and said to him, "I was fouled and we're in the bonus." He replied,

"No, it's side out. Get going." At that point, my coach called a timeout. I went over to the bench but no one could tell me why I wasn't being given the opportunity to shoot the foul shots. Coach drew up a quick play for me and we broke the huddle. We ran the play. The other team overplayed me and the ball was passed to one of my teammates who missed a shot at the buzzer. The game ended and we had lost.

As we left the court I learned that a Wyoming fan had thrown a cup on the floor near the end of the game and an official had blown his whistle just before I was fouled to remove the cup, even though it was on the opposite end of the floor. As you might imagine, I was upset. I wanted the opportunity to go to the foul line with the league championship on the line to make two foul shots for my teammates and coaches. I also wanted to prove to myself I could make them under great pressure in a hostile environment. Unfortunately, I never got the chance.

Ask your child how he or she would have felt if they had been in a similar situation? Would they have wanted to go to the foul line at the end of an important game with the chance to be the hero for the team or to be the goat? I loved situations like that where the pressure was intense. The heat of the kitchen warmed my heart.

I think that in such situations you see how tough a player is. When I say tough, I mean mentally tough. As I mentioned, there are two kinds of toughness in athletics: mental and physical. I might not have been the toughest guy physically, but mentally I was strong. I loved to be in situations that challenged me mentally.

Advise your young athlete that his mental toughness in a game-deciding situation—where he has the chance to win or lose a game—can determine the outcome of the game. Will he be firm like a rock or will he crumble like sand? Help him prepare to PUP—Perform Under Pressure.

MAKE THEM WHEN THEY COUNT

Some of the greatest players in the game, some who I would consider the most mentally tough players ever, have missed critical shots—shots that could have won games for their team. I think the difference between the mentally tough player and the average player is this: the mentally tough player wants to take the shot, and if he misses he is probably surprised because he fully expected to make it. The player who is not mentally tough might be surprised if the ball does go in because their expectation is failure. The mentally tough player's expectation is success in every situation.

A sad moment for me as a young boy was watching the Louisville Cardinals, my favorite team, go to the Final Four of the 1975 NCAA tournament. I watched as they played against UCLA in the semifinal game. Terry Howard stepped to the line with 20 seconds remaining in overtime with the opportunity to practically seal the victory for the Cardinals. At the time, Howard had not missed a foul shot the entire season—he was 28 for 28. That is quite an accomplishment. However, this time when he stepped to the line, he missed his first and second foul shots of that entire season. UCLA went on to beat my Cardinals. I felt sick.

Howard was able to shoot 28 foul shots during the course of that year without much pressure and he made all 28. But the foul shot that really takes the mental toughness is the one that is different—the one where the game could be on the line. In this case, the NCAA championship was on the line. Sadly for me, Terry, and his teammates, the shots did not go in.

On the other hand, I'll never forget watching Rumeal Robinson of Michigan, a 66% foul shooter on the season, hit two pressure foul shots to beat Seton Hall in the 1989 NCAA finals. He made both ends of a one and one with three seconds remaining in overtime to win the game, 80-79. It's hard for me to imagine a more pressure-packed situation in athletics than the one Rumeal found himself in back in 1989. He came through in the clutch and the Michigan fans will always love him for it.

THE INVITATION

Read the following letter to your child and ask him what he would do if this letter came in the mail to him.

Dear Athlete,

It has come to our attention that you have unusual athletic ability and that you have a love for sports. Our representatives in your city have seen you play and have recommended you as a candidate for our "Becoming an All-American" sports camp.

You can attend at no cost because we have received a government grant to conduct a sports camp in each of the 50 states. The camp in your state will begin July 9 and will conclude when the individual and camp goals have been achieved. This may take a week but may take up to four weeks. The camp will be held in the National Guard armory and on athletic fields located in your community. You will be housed in the barracks near the armory.

In order for you to attend, you will need to have written permission from your parents. They must give us, the camp directors, permission to push you to your limits and beyond. If they agree, have them sign the form included with this letter.

If you choose to come to the camp, it will be the most physically demanding experience you have ever had. However, we believe the results will do more for your chances to become an All-American than any other experience you will ever have. The two main instructors will be ex-marine sergeant Ray Robertson and Coach

Jim "Attack Dog" Johnson. In 20 years of coaching, Coach Johnson has produced 10 high school All-Americans and his teams have won seven state championships.

Sergeant Robertson was known during his 20-year Marine Corps career as the meanest drill sergeant to have ever served our country. He can shout louder and intimidate better than any man alive. He will be in charge of all aspects of your training other than the actual sports instruction.

Coach Johnson will handle the sports instruction. Today he is in perfect physical condition. During his college years, he was an All-American in two sports. The players he coached—those who stuck with his program—learned to love him even though there were many times when they felt that what he demanded was not worth the price they were made to pay.

Your daily schedule will begin each morning at 5:00 a.m. and will conclude each night at 11:00 p.m. There will also be some night exercises, which will be conducted at various times. A doctor will be on call to attend to extreme exhaustion and matters of physical and mental strain.

We advise you to be in excellent physical condition when you arrive. This will enable you to endure the first few days of excruciating physical and mental activities. You will, however, enjoy the food. Aside from that, you probably won't enjoy the other activities much, but later you will profit from the mental toughness you will gain, which will propel you to greatness.

Hope to see you there.

Sincerely,
The Selection Committee
"Becoming an All-American" Sports Camp

Ask your child, "Would you sign up for this camp? What if attending would be the only way you would be able to reach your full potential?"

Of course there is no such camp. So your child will have to find other situations that will stretch him to his limits and beyond. He will have to find other ways to increase his physical and mental toughness as he might have been able to at such a camp as the one I've described.

AIR FORCE CADETS ARE RODEO TOUGH

If I had to do it all over again, I think I would have applied to attend the Air Force Academy. I have always been fascinated by flying and the military concept of boot camp. I think one of the goals of that intense training is to make young men and women mentally tough. To put them in a situation where they are driven beyond their physical capabilities. To give them the challenge of keeping their cool with someone in their face screaming and yelling at them. The primary goal of these drill sergeants is to make their cadets mentally tough, to prepare them to go beyond their physical limits into the zone where they can develop a new level of mental toughness. The yelling and screaming are designed to force them to increase their mental strength in order to endure tremendous challenges.

In conditions such as boot camp and other pressure-packed situations, generally, two things happen: people either crumble like a sand castle being hit by a wave, or they stand like a rock. They either realize that they are just not ready for that kind of existence so they back away, or they draw on a mental toughness that enables them to endure to the end—to go beyond what they ever thought they could do physically and emotionally.

The Air Force Academy basketball team won the Mountain West Conference championship in 2004. They were not the most talented team in the league—not even close. What they were was a well-coached team made up of tough players, players that were physically and mentally as tough as they come.

PAY THE PRICE TO BE MENTALLY TOUGH

Maybe your son feels that he is mentally tough. On the other hand, maybe he is quite passive by nature. Tell your son that he can change his degree of mental toughness if he desires. If he would rather let someone else lead out and take the big shot, that is okay. On the other hand, if he wants to be rodeo tough and fiercely competitive, he can be. Developing mental toughness is a not an easy path to follow but everyone is invited to walk it if they choose to.

My path to mental toughness was not easy. My journey started many years ago with my older brother and our one-on-one games in the backyard. After repeated, heartbreaking losses, I would go in the house crying. That did little good, as my dad was not home and my mother had no sympathy for my plight. So my tears didn't help other than serving as an outlet for my pain.

After a time I would forget the agony that I had felt in the defeat, and my brother and I would be out there again, going at it like it was for the national championship. Again he would spot me an overwhelming lead and I would get my hopes up. But soon I would go down in flames. Finally, after many battles, my big brother found a friend his own age to play against and his interest in playing against me was over.

I am not sure I was competitive before those encounters with my older brother started. Looking back now, I must have been or else losing would not have been so painful. However, I know without a doubt that losing to him caused my desire to win and to be mentally tough to be far greater than it had ever been before.

ARE YOU PROTECTING YOUR CHILD?

You could have your son ride the bulls at the rodeo. Would you let him do that? What are you willing to allow him to do to become mentally tough? What do you do to help him to not crumble when the going is really tough and the pressure is on?

Are you allowing your child to be in difficult situations wherein he will develop a mental toughness that will make him as solid as a rock? Or are you protecting him from hardship and taking away opportunities to build mental toughness? I hope not.

I love to run with my kids. Running with them gives me an opportunity to help them go beyond their physical limits. Do what you can to put your children in situations that push them to their limits and allow them to stretch and grow.

THE FAMILY HIKE

One morning I decided to take my family on a hike up a nearby mountain. We took all six children ranging in ages from two to 16 at the time. Since some of them were so young, we decided on the relatively short one-and-a-half-hour hike to the large block letter "Y" on the mountain. With small children, I knew we would not likely make it all the way to the "Y" and that after we had walked for half-an-hour or so, the youngest ones would get tired. They would begin to complain and we would return to the bottom of the mountain. Because I didn't feel we would make it very far up the mountain, I did not bring any water.

To my surprise, a half-an-hour into the hike, all the children were enjoying the hike and we were making good progress up the mountain. Much later than I had predicted, the complaining started: "I'm thirsty. I'm tired." I took advantage of the situation and said, "All right, if that is the way you feel, let's head back down the mountain."

I was shocked when, almost in unison, everyone said, "No, no! We've got to finish the hike. We've got to make it to the Y." So we continued on. The sun was out and it was a hot day. I thought it was great that my kids wanted to keep going. I realized that we were in the midst of a great family experience in physical toughness, one that would soon turn into an experience in mental toughness. I said to myself, "Okay, let's see how they do without water."

We continued our wearied march up the mountain. The children, even the older ones, became more physically drained with each step. They felt even more thirsty and tired as the day warmed up. They complained but each of them wanted to keep moving toward our goal. At that point I started to feel uncomfortable with myself because I had not prepared for this hike with my wife and children and I felt their discomfort.

With strained expressions and slumped shoulders, they kept moving slowly up the mountain. I was tired myself because I was carrying my youngest child most of the way. Because of my lack of preparation, there was nothing I could do as their father to relieve their thirst and suffering. In a way, I am glad that was the case. I would have given them water if I had had it. It's hard for parents to see their children have to do hard things. We often want to step in to provide relief, even when sometimes we shouldn't.

I have never been more proud of my children than I was that day when we found ourselves in a situation that required them to be mentally and physically tough. I wanted to bail them out and go home so they wouldn't have to suffer. But they wanted to reach their goal and they did. Our family still remembers that day when we all went to the edge of our physical limits and entered into the zone of our mental limits. "The Hike" is now a treasured memory.

LET THEM PULL WEEDS

During the summer before Emily's ninth grade year, she was invited by the high school coach to go to a basketball camp in North Carolina. This coach was a very competitive and hard-working woman. She told the girls who wanted to be on her team that they would have to earn their own money to go on the trip. She wanted players that were both tough and skilled.

Emily seemed quite excited to earn money and pay her own way, and we thought it was great that she wanted to work and pay for the trip herself. We were grateful to the high school coach for inviting her and for helping these girls work to pay for the trip.

The coach found a job at a neighbor's house for my daughter and a teammate. The lot around the house was overgrown with weeds, and it was the girls' job to clear the weeds from the lot. I remember how excited I was when Emily came home that first afternoon exhausted because of the difficulty of pulling weeds all day. For the next two days she worked her heart out clearing weeds. Finally she reached what she felt was her physical limit. She was drained, sunburned, and ready to quit. She told me, "It's not worth it to pull all these weeds just to go to North Carolina."

I hurt for her. I was tempted to say, "You've made a good effort. If you want to quit you have my permission to do so." Instead I told her, "You started the job and agreed to finish it. You can't quit. You need to finish the job." She felt that I was asking too much. Nevertheless, the next day she returned to the unpleasant task. She continued to work hard. There was no more talk of quitting. She had gone beyond what she felt she could do but was still willing to do more. Later that day, sensing she had done enough and that a lesson had been fully learned, I went over and pulled weeds with her. Later, she enjoyed a great trip to North Carolina.

There may be times when you have to step in. However, try not step in too soon. Let your kids grow. It was a wonderful thing that this coach did for Emily. It helped her believe in her own capabilities. She overcame a large obstacle. This success in turn helped her to be a better basketball player.

THE BRICK WALK

I chose to do a project myself at one of my apartment complexes so that I could work beside my eleven-year-old son in building a brick walk. I wanted him to feel the spirit of working together with his Dad. I wanted to say and do things during our project to build his confidence and to teach him about hard work.

As can happen with work projects, this one took a little longer than we anticipated. We had to remove some dirt and then replace it with sand, which we could then level. Having finally completed this phase of the work, we started inserting the pavers in the walkway. After an hour or so of really hard work, we realized the temperature was over 100 degrees.

I hadn't foreseen that the project would take so long or that it would be as hot as it was. Again, like the family hike, I had failed to bring water. Physically it was a very demanding project. Ryan was hanging in there helping me with the bricks. We both started to get thirsty and fatigued. I could see he had about had it, and I felt like saying, "Let's call it a day. We can finish this another time."

But I didn't say that. I sensed we were in a great situation to learn a lasting lesson and I wanted to see how long he would go and not complain. He hung in there far longer than I would have expected.

We were probably into the project about three hours when we both wondered if we could do any more work in the heat of the day. However, we were getting close to the end and wanted to finish. About this time a girl came out of the apartment complex and offered us some water. Her kindness was well received. This gave us a little more energy and we were able to finish the project. Every time we drive by there now, Ryan always points out to the family, "Look! Right over there is the brick walk Dad and I made. It was hard and it was hot, but we did it."

RAISING BOYS

A story is told of a rich man who bought a farm. He did not want the land to raise crops, even though he did that. He wanted those acres to raise his boys. I wish we could all live and work on a farm. Farms generate work that produces the sort of sweat and strain that forms the ingredients of mental toughness. On a farm, you can't walk away and leave the cows unmilked or the chickens not fed or the hay bales in the field. You can't quit on a farm. What has to be done has to be done. There is no choice.

Hopefully, regardless of where you live, you will be able to teach your son or daughter to work hard by giving them challenging physical tasks to accomplish.

DEALING WITH NEGATIVITY FROM THE OPPOSITION

As your child begins to play in little leagues, sooner or later he is going to experience some taunting from an opponent or the opposing fans. You will have opportunities to coach him through how he reacts when someone from another team makes a negative comment, or when he hears someone in the stands say something negative about him.

You will have the opportunity to help him through that and give him the strength not to crumble. You can help him have the power to put it out of his mind.

LET YOUR ALL-AMERICAN
PLAY IN THE SNOW

Let's go back to the boy who was offended when I said that no one in his class would make it to the NBA. Three years after I gave that talk, I drove by and saw that young man playing basketball outside in a rainstorm. He was still there an hour later when I drove by again. I pulled over and said, "I live up the street a few blocks. I have an indoor gym if you want to get out of the rain and come over there and play." He looked at me, said thanks, and then turned and took another shot. Some time passed and one day this young man knocked on my door on a cold day wondering if he could do some shooting in my gym. I welcomed him in.

Later I wondered, "Did I do him a favor by inviting him to come and play in an easier place?" I'm not so sure.

There is something magical about pushing the snow off the court before you can play that makes the game all the sweeter. I remember, as a 14-year-old boy living in Kentucky, playing on our outdoor court with my friend Alex. Sometimes it would get so cold that my fingertips would split and bleed. I had to put Vaseline on them and wrap them in Band-aids so I could keep shooting. I'm glad my Mom didn't stop me from going out to shoot baskets when she saw me doctoring up my fingers. Fortunately, I was blessed with what I call "hard-road parents."

SOFT-ROAD PARENTS AND
HARD-ROAD PARENTS

As children grow from childhood to adulthood, they will have many positive experiences and successes. However, inevitably they will also face a variety of obstacles, emotional hardships, failures, and challenges.

All parents love the good times that come to their child and they respond in a similar positive manner. However, during the bad times the similarity in parental response is not there. As I have watched parents react to the bad or difficult times that come into their child's life, I have seen two distinct parental styles—soft-road parenting and hard-road parenting.

Soft-road parents want, with all their hearts, for their child to have a soft or an easy time as they travel along the "growing up" road. Soft-road parents always desire to be at the side of the child, holding his or her hand. When the child is about to fall, they reach out to catch him or they make sure that the child falls onto a soft surface so there is no pain felt. If an obstacle appears, these parents are quick to remove it so that the child's path is unobstructed. When storm clouds fill the sky, the soft-road parents appear with a coat and an umbrella to shield their child from the elements.

Their goal is to protect their child from any hurt or failure. They hurry to erase any uncomfortable challenge that comes into their child's life. They are quick to step in and do all they can to solve the child's problems. They are quick to blame others for any of their child's problems or shortcomings.

Soft-road parents are wonderful in their desires for their child, but I think they diminish their chances of achieving their goal of seeing their child mature into a successful, happy human being because they do what they can to remove all the opportunities for that to happen. Through their protective practices they lay the foundation for failure. When the time comes for the struggling child to walk the road of life alone, the soft-road parents watch with tears of disappointment and wonder who will help their child now as he or she stumbles into adulthood.

Hard-road parents also want, with all their hearts, for their child to have a painless journey to adulthood. They too desire to step in and shield any blows thrown at their child. However, instead of rushing in, they stand nearby (sometimes in tears) to watch how their child will fare on his or her own. They restrain themselves as they realize the value of a child first doing all within his or her power to resolve difficulties.

Standing back and allowing a child to struggle through some of life's challenges is not easy for any parent. It is much easier to "hover over" and "rush in." However, hard-road parents know that opposition is the foundation of strength.

Hard-road parents occasionally walk at the side of their child. However, when conditions are safe, under the watchful eye of the parent, the child is usually free to walk alone, even more so as the child matures. With such freedom, the child will, at times, stumble and skin a knee. These parents, seeing the mishap, will restrain the urge to "rush in," knowing that the child will pick himself up and by so doing learn to avoid future falls. The hard-road parents will give counsel to their child on how to overcome future obstacles. When obstacles appear on the hard road, the parents are aware; however, they stand back and the child is allowed to figure out a way to personally overcome the obstacle. They give the child time to find, on his or her own, the best way to go over, around, or through the obstacle.

When the skies fill with ominous weather, these parents give encouragement, yet they allow the child to do whatever is necessary to find the needed shelter. As much as is possible and wise, the hard-road parents will stand back just a bit and allow their child to feel the heartache and pain of failure. They don't immediately step in to try to make everything better. They share in the child's pain. However, their support is tempered by their understanding that growth can come from adversity.

And lastly, the hard-road parents teach their child accountability. They understand that young people create many of their own problems and should be held accountable for such. By not rushing in to rescue the child, these parents teach their child to be responsible for his or her own actions.

Unlike the "soft-road parents," the "hard-road parents" will eventually have the opportunity to watch their child come to the end of the hard road. They will embrace each other and smile proudly, and with joy in their hearts, watch as their child walks firmly into adulthood prepared for the challenges ahead.

THE HARD ROAD OF ATHLETICS CREATES RODEO TOUGHNESS

Athletic competition will require your child to walk down a hard road. Don't spend your time trying to soften the experience for him or her. There will be "trying times" when it will be very difficult to restrain yourself from rushing in to rescue your child. Restrain yourself anyway. By allowing your child to walk the hard road, or in other words, to develop a little "rodeo toughness," he or she will be better prepared for the tough challenges of sports and for the even tougher challenges of life after sports.

DEVIN DURRANT'S
ALL-AMERICAN PUZZLE

PART 6
DARE MIGHTY THINGS

SELF-CONFIDENCE

In our home there is a saying on the wall of the children's laundry room that says "Dare Mighty Things" in big bold letters. A child must feel some self-confidence in order to want to dare mighty things. The full quote is from Theodore Roosevelt and reads: "Far better it is to Dare Mighty Things, to win glorious triumphs even though checkered by failures, than to take rank with those poor spirits who neither enjoy much nor suffer much because they live in the grey twilight that knows not victory or defeat."

As a parent, you don't want your children to live in the "grey twilight." You want them to experience the thrill of victory. To make that happen your young athlete has to believe in himself.

Confidence, or a belief in one's self, activates all the other parts of the All-American Puzzle. Confidence causes an athlete to love a challenge. Confidence causes an athlete to dare mighty things such as trying out for the junior high team, striving to win a place on the starting five, stopping the opposition from scoring, taking the ball strong to the basket, trying to make the high school varsity team as a sophomore, or working to get a college scholarship.

Charles Barkley, an All-American and a great All-Pro, had the confidence to dare mighty things. He reveals his feelings of confidence by saying:

> There might be two or three guys as good as me, but nobody's better than me. . . . Of course you need the talent to do it, but talent isn't the only ingredient. If you don't feel that way, if you don't think you're better than everybody else, you can't be better. . . . It's absolutely necessary to have that attitude. When you realize it and can back it up, at that point you just have to get out of your own way.[1]

The confident athlete gets out of his own way by believing in himself. He has the confidence he can conquer the mighty challenges of today and tomorrow.

Becoming a great athlete is a process of having the confidence to go from one challenge to a greater one. It is like a cycle leading ever upward.

THE ALL-AMERICAN CYCLE

This cycle can be seen clearly in the challenge that comes from continually playing against better players. This is called "playing up." I learned that athletes experience a cycle when they are playing with better players. I call it the All-American Cycle. It goes like this:

First, when you are playing against older, bigger, stronger, faster, and more experienced players, you feel uncomfortable and intimidated. This is the "I don't belong with these guys" phase. This is not a particularly enjoyable phase of the All-American Cycle.

After some time, if you have the confidence to stick with it, you will begin to feel like you do belong with the older guys. You will start to feel comfortable and your confidence will begin to increase. This is the "I do belong with these guys" phase.

Time passes and you enter the "I'm better than most of these guys" phase. You no longer feel intimidated at all. This phase is a lot of fun.

The final phase is the "graduation phase." It is at this point that you realize you are one of the best players in the group and that you need to find a new group of players that bring you back to those feelings of "I don't belong with these guys." The cycle then repeats itself. You continue to dare mighty things.

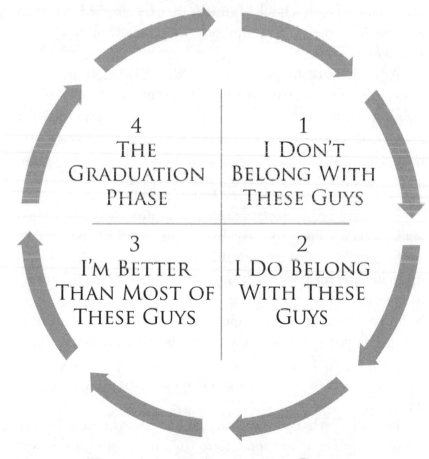

| 4 THE GRADUATION PHASE | 1 I DON'T BELONG WITH THESE GUYS |
| 3 I'M BETTER THAN MOST OF THESE GUYS | 2 I DO BELONG WITH THESE GUYS |

THE ALL-AMERICAN CYCLE

For many people, it is easiest to just avoid this cycle and not enter in where you feel uncomfortable. But if you don't have the courage and confidence to meet tough challenges, you will never become a great player. Great players love a challenge. When you are coaching yourself, you must constantly search for a greater challenge.

Sometimes that next challenge is built into the system. A good example of that is the professional baseball system. Baseball players go through the All-American Cycle from the beginning to the end of their careers. There always seems to be a new challenge. It goes like this. A good baseball player is drafted out of high school. He might then be assigned to play in a Single A league. As he progresses, he is moved up to Double A and then Triple A.

At each level, he goes through the All-American Cycle. When he enters the "graduation phase" of the All-American Cycle in Triple A, he is called up to the major leagues—the pinnacle of baseball. He then begins the All-American Cycle for the last time.

THE VISION OF THE FUTURE

Your child's life story may or may not have been filled with successes along the way. He might have little or no self-confidence. He may have a multitude of memories that all add up to his present positive or negative feelings about his ability to meet challenges and to be a winner. Whatever the case may be for your youngster, it is important for him, and you, to know that, as Stephen R. Covey says in his best-selling book, *The 7 Habits of Highly Effective People*:

"The vision of the future can overcome the baggage of the past."

No matter what your child's past has caused him to believe about himself, it is not too late to turn things around. It will take some time, obstacles will appear, but it can be done.

DON'T LET TEMPORARY FAILURE
ERODE YOUR CONFIDENCE

Every new challenging goal and situation will have within itself the destructive seeds of self-doubt. Help your child to be strong when self-doubt comes. Let him know even professional athletes at times go into slumps that damage their confidence. Help him work his way through it. While he is young, his confidence will require effort from both you and him.

That brings to mind a particular teammate I had in college. He was a great player, a particularly good shooter, but for one reason or another he lost confidence in his shot. He suffered through a difficult stretch. Finally, the coaches cured him by putting together a highlight video of him making baskets. They wanted to put successful images in his mind—the ball going through the hoop time after time. After that "confidence booster" session he was able to get his shot back and return to the player he had been before he lost his confidence.

I remember times as an athlete, particularly in the NBA, when self-doubt would creep into my mind. I would start questioning my abilities. After my time in the NBA, I went to Spain to play. The first year, playing near Barcelona, I felt comfortable from the beginning. I was playing good basketball and I had a good year. My second year, playing with a new team near Madrid, I struggled in the first few games of the pre-season. I could sense my teammates were doubting the abilities of their new teammate. It finally got to the point that the team leader came to me and said, "We need you. You need to get going."

That next game I hit a few shots and started feeling good. My teammates got me the ball and I couldn't miss—I scored over 30 points that night. I could see in my teammates' eyes, "Hey, we've got something here. This guy can play."

I think we are all a bit dependent on those around us and what we think they think of us. I had gotten the feeling that my teammates thought I was a failure, but then I could see the transformation in them when I went out and played the way I was supposed to be playing. Attitudes changed—their attitude toward me and my attitude toward myself. From that point on my teammates and I had a successful season.

As your son matures, the sooner he can learn to bounce back from bouts of self-doubt the better off he will be. Tennis legend John McEnroe said:

> I firmly believe that one of the hallmarks of a champion—any champion—is the ability to absorb losses and regain confidence immediately.[2]

USE FAILURE AS FUEL

We have all heard the story about Michael Jordan getting cut from his high school team. Here is the rest of the story, as told by David Halberstam:

> The summer after ninth grade, Jordan and Smith both. . . [tried] out for the varsity as sophomores, Smith because he was six foot six, Jordan because he was so quick. . . . But on the day the varsity cuts were announced—it was the big day of the year, for they had all known for weeks when the list would be posted—he and Roy Smith had gone to the Laney gym.
>
> Smith's name was there. Jordan's was not. Michael was of course bitterly disappointed. But he did not retreat. His failure fueled his motivation. He charged ahead and was so dominant as a JV player that the varsity players started coming early just to see him play.
>
> Michael's supposed failure spurred him on, according to those who watched him play thereafter. Leroy Smith noticed that while Jordan had been wildly competitive before he had been cut, after the cut he seemed even more competitive than ever, as if determined that it would never happen again.[3]

Every athlete at one time or another has to deal with failure. The great athletes build on failure. They use it to climb to greater heights.

DON'T BE AFRAID TO TAKE A RISK

Teach your son to be a smart risk-taker. It is okay to miss a shot or make a bad pass. I like what coach John Wooden said about taking risks:

> I constantly repeated to my teams the admonition I had learned from Piggie Lambert at Purdue: "The team that makes the most mistakes will probably win." There is much truth in that statement if you analyze it properly. The doer makes mistakes, and I wanted doers on my team—players who made things happen.[4]

Michael Jordan offers this advice to those who are afraid to take a risk:

> I've missed more than nine thousand shots in my career. I've lost almost three hundred games. Twenty-six times I've been trusted to take the game-winning shot and missed. I've failed over and over and over again in my life, and that is why I succeed.[5]

One of the sweetest moments I ever experienced as an athlete was winning the Utah basketball high school state championship. In each of the two prior years we had lost to Danny Vranes and his Skyline teammates in the tournament semifinals on last-second shots. But those failures served to make our state championship victory even sweeter.

THE BLOCKED SHOT

It takes confidence for a young athlete to want to "play up." At first your child will feel intimidated. He will feel that he doesn't belong. He may have to learn some tough lessons. Let me tell you about a lesson I was taught the hard way while "playing up."

Between my junior and senior years of high school, I could have enjoyed the comfort of playing all summer in the Provo High gym against my high school teammates, but in doing that I would never have had the humbling experience I had one day at the Marriott Center, at Brigham Young University, playing against some members of the BYU team.

I remember one time when I drove the baseline and went up to dunk the ball. BYU had a big six-foot ten-inch center named Alan Taylor. Alan jumped up and put his hand on the ball and cleanly blocked me from dunking it.

I was so embarrassed that my dunk shot had been blocked that I called a foul on Alan. He glared at me. He knew it wasn't a foul, and the other players knew it wasn't a foul, and I knew it wasn't a foul. I was being recruited by BYU at the time and all the players knew it. For that reason they were nice enough to me that they gave me the ball back in order to help me minimize my embarrassment.

It was that experience and others that helped me realize that if I was going to dunk the basketball at the next level, I was going to have to jump a little bit higher or be a little bit quicker. That is a lesson I would not have learned playing with my high school friends.

EMBARRASSMENT IS PART OF PLAYING UP

Yes, I was embarrassed a lot of times as a high school player by the college guys. That happens when you are playing against superior competition. The embarrassment that came with playing with guys who were better than me made me determined to improve. That was one of the blessings of being able to play against college competition while in high school. It forced me to improve. There weren't many guys in my high school league that could have blocked a dunk. It was a great advantage for me to be able to play with college players the entire summer and early fall before starting my high school senior season.

FIND A POSITIVE

Speaking of getting my shot blocked, I had a lot of experience with that. It all started when I played, as a young boy, against my brother who was four years older and much taller than me. For many years, I played one-on-one against him. When I was young, it was very difficult for me to make a basket because he would block my shot. Growing up I got my shot blocked hundreds of times by him. That forced me to develop moves to free myself so that I could get my shot off against a taller opponent. Those games against my older brother did a lot to make me competitive and to improve my game.

The interesting thing to me about those early days when I had my shot blocked so often was it taught me an important lesson. I remember many times in high school and college getting my shot blocked, but by that time I knew how to handle it. I would just grab the ball and go back up again and either make the shot or make the shot and get fouled. I had come to realize that there is no harm in getting your shot blocked. It's what happens *after* you get your shot blocked that counts. I learned that many times when a player blocks your shot, he relaxes and feels good about himself. In that instant, you can grab the ball and go back up again and make a basket.

Good lessons can be learned from negative experiences. Help your son learn from his experiences, both positive and negative.

JIMMY MARSHALL'S COURT

Between my eighth and ninth grade year in junior high, my older brother, Matt, was between his junior and senior year of high school. One day he invited me to come along with him to

play basketball at Jimmy Marshall's house. Jimmy Marshall's
dad wanted his son to be able to work on his game close to
home so he built a full-length basketball court in the lot next
to his house.

When we arrived I noticed that many of the guys that
would make up the Seneca High School basketball team that
fall were there—Leonard and Stuart Olsen, David Jones,
Jimmy Marshall, and others. I was welcomed as "a tenth man
insurance policy." That meant that I would sit and watch until
someone had to leave and then I would be the tenth man. First,
I watched. Eventually, I got to play. It was a great thing for a
"soon-to-be-ninth-grader" to play with varsity players. As I
played with these guys, I knew I didn't belong.

My hope was simply not to make any mistakes. I knew I
wasn't supposed to shoot. I was there to rebound, pass, and
defend as best I could. I also felt like a punching bag when I
played with these guys. They never tried to take it easy on the
youngest player.

Fortunately for me, I got to play at Jimmy Marshall's court
several times that summer. I took my share of abuse from the
older guys, but over time I earned their respect. I was even
allowed to take some shots in the games—as long as they went
in the basket. From the end of that summer on, I had some
older friends at the high school who were always looking out
for me. Thank goodness for an older brother who was willing
to drag me along as a "tenth man insurance policy." And thank
goodness for a dad like Mr. Marshall who wanted to create a
place where young men could congregate to improve themselves
as basketball players.

PLAY IN THE OLDER LEAGUE

That same year I had another experience that helped
toughen me up and give me confidence. My church decided
to enter a community basketball league. My church team was

short of players so I got to suit up with guys three and four years older than me. It was fun competing with older teammates who covered up for my mistakes while encouraging me when I did something well.

Of course, my older brother was there to protect me from trouble and to pat me on the back when I did something good. He was more than willing to beat on me when we played one-on-one, but when we were teammates, he would look out for me and encourage me.

I also had the chance to play for Steve White, our church team coach. Nobody wanted to win more than Steve White. He had a big, competitive heart and he expected his players to give everything they had when they were on the floor. He also wasn't shy about letting the officials know how he felt about their performance. I will never forget the time Coach White tossed a chair across the gym floor and promptly got tossed out of the building. And this was long before Bob Knight did the same thing.

Playing with the older guys helped me to believe I had something to offer the team. I started out in the "I-don't-belong-with-these-guys" phase and over time entered the "I-belong-with-these-guys" phase. I started to believe that I was a good basketball player.

MAKE FRIENDS WITH THE "GYM RATS"

The off-season gives a player the opportunity to spend time with the gym rats. When your child is in junior high encourage him to make friends with the gym rats. The rats are those who may not have made it in college, but felt like they were better than those who did. They know they have no future in the game—their day has passed or they may just be trying to stay in good physical condition. Gym rats come in all shapes and sizes. They love to play ball. One of my favorites was a short pharmaceutical salesman. He worked until three in the afternoon each day. Then he would come to the gym. He lived for his gym time. He and I became good friends.

I also loved to play with football players who were looking for some physical activity during the off-season. One guy, Brad Oates, played in the NFL. He sure knew how to set a pick and he had a pretty decent jumper. Pete Van Valkenberg was another gym rat who was fun to have as a teammate. He was a good basketball player who also had led the country in rushing during his college football playing days at BYU.

I particularly enjoyed playing with the Samoans and Tongans. They were great teammates because they had such a passion for winning and they were fearless.

Recently, I crossed paths with one of my old university English professors. He reminded me of the summer before my sophomore year of high school when I would go to the BYU Fieldhouse and stand around until he and the other older guys—most of them university professors—needed another body and they would invite me to join them. Most of them were not great players but for a young kid like me they were the perfect competition at that stage of my life. My game improved dramatically playing with those guys. I didn't know anyone and it took courage to be there. I felt intimidated, but I was there. Over time I felt right at home with my new group of friends. I treasure my days as a young athlete playing with the gym rats with all their different shapes, colors, sizes, and personalities.

THEY WILL NEED YOU SOONER OR LATER

Encourage your son to go where the older guys are playing. At first they will ignore him. After a while someone will have to go home. They will look at your son and invite him in. It always happens that way. A universal rule in the world of pickup games is that if you hang around long enough, someone will have to leave and you will be there to take his place.

Tell your future All-American that when he is young and in a game with older guys, to get the ball to them. Get rebounds and hustle after loose balls. Be a team player. These things will endear your child to them and they will start to look out for him on the court.

EXCUSE ME

When I came back to Utah from Kentucky, I was a sophomore but I had the opportunity to practice with the juniors and seniors on the varsity team at Provo High. This was a good chance to improve my game by practicing each day with these older players. They were hard on me. I was a threat to their minutes. I could have shied away from these older guys but I was determined to compete with them.

One day an opponent set a screen on me. I was determined to fight my way through it. As I did so, I said, "Excuse me." The older guys heard what I had said and began to laugh. Practice came to a halt because they couldn't stop laughing. Yes, I was quite embarrassed, but life went on. It was just another tough moment for me as I worked through the All-American Cycle.

That year made all the difference for me. I played on the sophomore and JV teams in the games but my improvement that year came when I had opportunities to play against the varsity players in practice. That year of "practicing up" against some excellent high school players made my junior and senior year very productive.

AVOID COMPLACENCY

When your child enters the All-American Cycle, he will begin by playing against superior competition. At first he will feel intimidated. Then he will gain competence and confidence and will begin to feel comfortable. Playing up is a principle of improving for the struggling player and the star player. The struggling player is usually more humble and is willing to do all he can to improve.

The star player has a different challenge. Such players become satisfied and think they have arrived. They rest on their achievements. They are comfortable with where they are. Such players need to play up and become not only the best on their team but the best they can possibly be. Don't fall into the trap of contentment that Coach Pitino describes:

> I continue to be amazed by how many players become complacent as soon as they start to have some success. One of my players will be on the second team, and he will work incredibly hard in practice, sometimes even fanatically so, to get into that starting five and have his name announced at the start of a game. This is his goal, and he will do just about anything to reach it, pay any price. Often, it's something he's been striving for since he picked up his first basketball. Then he finally gets there. And what happens? He doesn't play as hard in practice anymore. He's become content. I just don't understand it. People achieve success. Then they stop working. It's as if success were the kiss of death.[6]

If your child starts to feel complacent, he needs to work harder and challenge himself to improve by playing against the best competition you and he can find. Not only will your child's skills increase, but his desire to win will become greater.

PLAYING UP REQUIRES COURAGE

Kobe Bryant played against older guys a lot as a young man. The true measure of Kobe's potential came not at summer camps, or in tournaments, or when he was playing against other kids his age, but in pickup games with some of the best athletes on the planet. It was shortly after his junior year in high school when Kobe first received permission from John Lucas, who was then coach of the Philadelphia 76ers, to work out with his team. Kobe was just a skinny 16 year old at the time, but it didn't take long for him to prove that he could hold his own against NBA talent.

Ask your child, "Would you dare to compete with NBA players as a 16 year old?" or " How about playing against high school varsity players when you are in the ninth grade?" It takes courage, but entering the All-American Cycle is the best way to overcome fear and improve one's game.

The greatest female soccer player in the world, Mia Hamm, had the courage to enter the All-American Cycle by playing up against some of the best soccer players in the world at age 15:

> . . . In international play, every player was fast and strong, and many had more experience than Mia. In order to make certain her game continued to develop to its full potential, Dorrance [her coach] realized he had to expose Mia to the level of play practiced by the United States national team. He asked her to participate in an upcoming training camp and try out for the team. Even if she didn't make it, she would learn what it would take for her game to reach the next level.

> Mia agreed. She was excited by the opportunity Dorrance provided, but she was also apprehensive. Most other team members were either in college or had recently graduated. Mia Hamm was only 15 years old. She was nervous, shy, and a little intimidated. All of a sudden she was supposed to play with players such as striker Michelle Akers, who many people considered to be the best women's soccer player in the world. At Mia's first meeting with the team, they all spent several hours in the gym, working out with weights and other fitness equipment.

> Mia had never spent much time in the gym before. She'd just played soccer. The long workout left her exhausted. "I thought I'd die," she remembered later.

Then she got the surprise of her young life. After working out in the gym, the squad headed outside for practice! She spent another two hours on the field, going through drills and scrimmages with the team. At the end of the day, all she wanted to do was sleep. Her thighs throbbed, and she felt as if her entire body was going to go into one huge cramp. She had never worked so hard in her life.

Yet she couldn't keep her eyes closed. Every time she did, she saw herself playing soccer on the national team. She was more excited about the game than she had ever been before. The players on the team were so good, they made Mia reassess her entire approach to soccer.

The experience made a lasting impression on Mia. Thus far, soccer had been important to her and she had cared about winning or losing, but she had never felt that losing was the end of the world. As a female athlete, she had been conditioned to care less about winning than male athletes did.

On the national team, everything was different. "I loved how competitive it was," she said later. " I was like, 'Wow. Look how hard these players work.'" The captain of the national team, April Heinrichs, made a particular impression on Hamm. "She just wanted to win, and for a female wanting that, it was just so new. I realized I had to do a lot of stuff on my own if I wanted to stay on this team."[7]

"Playing up" for Mia was a mind-expanding experience. It changed both the way she viewed the game and the way she prepared to compete.

LIKE A MAN

As a small boy, I didn't need my dad to teach me how to dribble, pass, rebound, and shoot. But I sure needed him to help me feel good about myself.

As a father you can have a profound influence on your child's confidence. You want to give him so many things and opportunities. You work hard to provide food and shelter for him. Yet that which will be of greatest worth to him is your affirmation to him that he is a very important person and that he is capable of excelling in many ways.

I remember many times while I was working side by side with my dad on any number of different projects, he would say to me, "Devin, having you help me is like having a man." Each time he said that it had the same impact. His positive words made me feel good about myself. Even at that young age I was smart enough to realize I wasn't doing the work that a man could do. However, my father's words overrode all logic and made me feel confident. What he said made me want to work harder—to be more like a man. He made me feel like I had something to contribute, not only to the task we were working on, but in all aspects of my life.

Dad and I often played basketball together on our homemade court. The most valuable lesson he taught me was his assurance each time we played that I was a young All-American in the making. During my boyhood and later in my college career, he was always more than generous in his praise. As we played basketball or football or baseball, he helped me believe that I was a very capable athlete. You, as a parent, more than any other person, are the mirror into which your child looks to determine his self-worth.

I DID IT!

I remember when my dad invented a game to help his children feel self-worth. I strongly recommend this game to you mothers and fathers of small children. In my home as I grew up, we had a tradition of gathering for some family time once a week; naturally, our family gathering included some time for games. My favorite game was the "I Did It" game. It was a simple game that went as follows: Dad would speak to me or one of my siblings and say, "Go into my bedroom and get a pair of socks out of my drawer and then go to the front door and knock on it three times and then go into the kitchen and open and close the refrigerator door. After you have done all that, come back into this room and do a somersault and then hand the socks to me and say, 'I did it!'"

I loved to take my turn. Each time the tasks varied but you always ended the game by saying, "I did it!" Playing that game always gave me a feeling of accomplishment. I loved getting all the tasks done right and reporting my success to my parents and receiving their congratulations. That game is now played enthusiastically by the next generation.

HOME INSULATION

One of the great luxuries of the home is that it can be insulated from society. As your child gets older, society can be tough both mentally and emotionally. Home is the place to patch him up. Home is the place to immunize him against self-doubt. Your praise can have a powerful effect on his belief in himself. You should constantly remind yourself that out of small things such as a positive comment here and there, can come mighty things such as self-confidence and success.

At report card time, my wife and I praise our children for their scholastic successes. We don't give them any monetary rewards for their accomplishments in school, but we praise them abundantly. Along with the praise we offer them a hug and a kiss for each "A" on their report card. They always let us know that they would prefer cash over a hug and a kiss, but someday they will see how much more valuable praise and a hug and a kiss is for a child than money.

Out in society your children will have plenty of opportunities to fail, to be criticized, and to be kicked around emotionally. As parents we need to more than balance the scales upon which they will weigh their self-worth against their self-doubt by showing them that we believe in them. Remember confidence, like good bread, is homemade.

Prayer can also aid your young athlete in having positive feelings about himself. Most agree that God doesn't care who wins a ball game. However, all would agree He cares about your child as an individual and as an athlete. Teach your child to let Him help.

YOUR ROLE CHANGES

In sports, as in all aspects of life, there comes a time when your child must step out of the home and into the world. The competitive forces of the world then have a profound influence on your son's belief in himself. His peers, his coaches, and others will exert a tremendous influence on him. His successes and failures will register deeply in his heart. As much as a child might believe in himself because of a positive parent, that confidence may be destroyed if he goes outside of the home and meets criticism after criticism, and failure after failure. During the transition time of going from the emotional safety of the home to the insecurity of the world, the parent's role is to be a safe harbor to which the boy can return for support.

It is very difficult to totally counteract negative opposition. However, you do have some control. You have a responsibility to know your child, to know whether he responds to criticism or to praise, and how he is best motivated. When you look at the coaches that your son will be playing for you should factor this information into the equation. Do some research on a coach, or a teacher, or other adults that you know are going to have some influence on your child. Find out what approach these people are going to take as they work with your son. You can then be a facilitator to help create optimal opportunity for enough success to maintain, and hopefully add to, your son's self-esteem.

If you are unable to handpick your son's coach, which is usually the case during the early years, help him make the most of the situation he is in. Be ready to help him understand the positive and the negative of the situation and give him the support he will need to stick with it and to grow.

FROM "HANDS ON" TO "HEARTS ON"

Once I began junior high, my father's role was mostly that of a positive observer. Before each game during warmups, I loved to look into the stands and make sure my dad was there. I enjoyed having him come to see me play. After each game, he and I would spend time talking about the game. He was always positive with his comments. In almost any competition there is something positive that you can emphasize. I think part of being a parent is being selective in the comments you make. Are they constructive or destructive? During my junior high days, my dad's primary role became that of a cheerleader. That is what I needed from him. I didn't need my dad to tell me, "You've got to block out better and get more rebounds." I didn't need him criticizing my teammates or my coach. I just needed a dad who cared about me and was supportive.

I'll never forget the Christmas gift my dad gave me during my junior year in high school. I had to look in the freezer to see what it was. His gift to me was 15 beefsteaks—one for each pre-game meal for the remaining games on our schedule. From this I knew my dad cared about me and wanted me to succeed.

My mother was also supportive in her own way. She was the one who would drive me to and from practice although I don't remember her coming to any of my games before high school. She was so busy raising eight children that she had almost no free time. As I improved in high school, my name began to appear in the local newspaper. After she read my name in the newspaper, she figured she ought to go see what her son was up to. By that time my siblings were older and she had more free time. From then on, she hardly ever missed a game—I was her favorite player! And yes, she was my favorite fan.

EARLY SUCCESS HELPS

Let's hope that your child will have enough early success in sports that his self-confidence will thrive. Learn what you can about how well your son is doing on the elementary school playground and in neighborhood games. Occasionally, play with him to see how he is progressing.

I remember how good it felt to play kick ball in elementary school. When it was my turn to kick, my classmates moved back. I also enjoyed a game called *pomp*, in which I would run from one side of the field to the other as people tried to tackle me. I was usually one of the last ones tackled. I would come home at night and tell my dad about my early sports successes, and he would be as happy as I was about them.

MY GREATEST THRILL IN SPORTS

When I was 10 years old, I was playing Little League baseball, pitching to a 12 year old—one of the best players in the league. He hit a line drive that hit me in the chest, knocked the wind out of me, and knocked me down. I crawled over, grabbed the baseball, stood up, threw it to first base, and collapsed. My coaches and my dad came out to the mound, picked me up, wiped the tears out of my eyes, and dusted me off. I caught my breath again, let the pain subside, and was able to continue pitching.

The biggest thrill I ever felt in my sports career came a few weeks later. The tables were turned and I was batting against this same kid who had earlier drilled me with the line drive. He threw me a fast ball and I hit it over the fence. I have a vivid memory of ecstatically running the bases. It was my first home run in Little League. I was jumping up and down with joy as I ran around the bases. What a great feeling that was to face my fears and hit a home run off someone who was considered one of the best pitchers in the league. That had a profound influence on my confidence.

I WAS NOT CHOSEN

As a fourth grader, my confidence prompted me to want to play with the older guys. After school I often played basketball with some fifth and sixth graders. One day eleven of us showed up to play. We started choosing sides. Being younger than the others, I was a little nervous as to whether or not I was going to get chosen. I knew the plan was to play five-on-five, but with eleven guys I knew someone would be watching from the sidelines. I stood as tall as I could and tried to look athletic. Eventually, both captains had chosen their four teammates. I was not chosen. They moved to one side of the court to begin the game. I stood on the other side, all by myself. I felt rejected. I felt like a failure. I started to cry. By this time these guys and I had become pretty good friends. Seeing me cry, they decided to play six-on-five that day so that I could play. I appreciated their kindness but my self-confidence took a big blow that day.

I don't remember telling my father about that day. Someday your son will suffer in silence. Try to stay close to him emotionally so he will feel your support in spite of his discouragement.

THE PROMOTION

When I was in third grade, I had a teacher who helped me to believe in myself. Mrs. Matthews helped me feel like I was a good student. Because I was able to finish my assignments faster than the other kids, she gave me other challenging projects to work on. In the middle of the year, she asked me if I wanted to go up to the fourth grade and participate in some classes there. I agreed. I started taking one class in the fourth grade, then two, and then three. After a time, the principal called my mom and dad, Mrs. Matthews, and me into his office for a conference and asked if I would be interested in moving from the third grade to the fourth grade in the middle of the school year. It seemed like a good idea to me and it seemed like a good idea to my parents. So the next week I became part of the fourth grade. It was a little unsettling at first being with all these new, older kids, but in time I felt comfortable. Through that experience, I felt like people believed in me—my third-grade teacher, my principal, my fourth-grade teacher, and my parents all believed in me. Having all those adults show confidence in me made me feel great.

My father could have said, "No, I don't want my son moving up a grade. That will be a disadvantage for him in sports." Actually, the knowledge that he and my mother and others believed in me had a greater influence on me as an athlete than delaying my high school graduation a year might have had.

With these kind of experiences, I felt pretty good about myself as a young kid. I began to feel I could succeed in anything that I pursued. You can give that same feeling to your child.

PLAY WITH YOUR CHILD

You may or may not be a good athlete yourself, but even if you aren't, your size gives you an insurmountable advantage over your child. So, playing against you will give him his first opportunity to "play up."

My father fancied himself as quite a good basketball player. When I was little we would play one-on-one and he would beat me good. As I grew, our games became closer. Then I reached the point that I could beat him. So he started to be both the opposition and the referee. He called a pretty one-sided game and won for awhile. Then I got so I could beat him even with the referee on his side. From that point on our competition was limited to shooting games and he never stopped being a difficult opponent in those games. We had a lot of fun during those father-son battles.

My sons, Ryan and Joseph, have played a lot of one-on-one and shooting games with me over the years. Joseph, at nine years old, is still a bit young for much of a one-on-one game but we have had some good games of h-o-r-s-e. Ryan, at 13 years of age, is a fun opponent. There have been times when I let him get close to beating me. However, I always made sure that I beat him. I wanted him to feel as though I was someone who was very difficult to defeat. Then, when the time came that he did beat me, it would be a real accomplishment for him.

I have always tried to play him in a way that was fun for him. I didn't want to make it so he didn't want to play because he always lost. I would congratulate him on the good things that he did. I would tell him that I sure hoped he wouldn't beat me the next time we played. I would talk at the dinner table to the family about how good he was getting and how close he came to beating me and announce that it would not be long until he would get his first victory over me. I wouldn't block all his shots even though I could have. I blocked just enough of his shots so he would know he had to try harder. We always had fun.

As he got older, I had to try harder and harder because he kept getting better and better. However, I still didn't want to let him win because I wanted him to continue to work toward that goal.

When he was about eleven and a half years old, we were playing to seven baskets. He was up five baskets to three. If I was going to beat him, I knew it was time for me to get going. I defended him closely. However, he made a quick move and scored—six to three. I figured I better turn it up a notch defensively to stop this little eleven-and-a-half-year-old. He drove toward me. I covered him tightly. He surprised me by spinning around and throwing up a wild hook shoot. I lunged as high as I could to block it, but I was just a little too far away from him. The ball arched up just beyond my extended fingers and swished through the net. My son had won! On that last point, I was trying as hard as I could, but he had beaten me fair and square. It was a real triumph for him. I was probably more thrilled than he was by his victory. It was fun to see him beat his dad. In a few years, I expect Ryan to be able to beat his dad on a regular basis.

PLAYING UP AT HOME

As I write this book in 2005, my son, Ryan, is 13 years old. I am always looking for opportunities for him to play up. We just moved to a new neighborhood where there are boys a bit older than he is who love sports. I encourage him to make friends with these older boys in hopes that he will have opportunities to compete against them. A friend his own age and talent level who loves basketball would also be a great asset to him.

If your child is not as good as the other guys his age, then playing with them will be uncomfortable. Encourage him to keep at it. With time, improvement will come. If your son continues to play against those who are better than he is and then practices on his own, he will soon catch up to them. In time, he will pass them, and then he will need to find new opportunities to play against a superior opponent.

As I have said, I used to play against my older brother a lot. Recently, we determined that the win-loss record for all those games was about 963 wins and one loss for him and one win and 963 losses for me. That win-loss record doesn't matter now but it certainly did then. I hated to lose to my brother. But, in fact, I wasn't the loser. I was the winner. I was given opportunity after opportunity to compete against a superior opponent.

Teach your child that when he "plays up" it may take time, but eventually he will get a win. When he does, he will have another piece to place in his All-American Puzzle.

FROM FAILURE TO
SUCCESS AS A FATHER

When Ryan signed up as a ten-year-old for his first year of Little League baseball, I made the false assumption that he was comfortable with baseball because he had been playing with his friends on the playground and after school. I was wrong. When the games started, I quickly realized that he did not understand the basic fundamentals of the game. No one had ever taught him to hit, to field, or to throw, and he hadn't learned it in the neighborhood. I could see that he didn't have much confidence as a baseball player. When he would go to bat he would swing with what I would call a "swing and a prayer." He had no confidence, no belief that he could hit the ball.

That first year of Little League baseball was one bad experience after another. His team ended the season in last place. At the end of the year Ryan felt like a failure. I felt like a failure also because as a father I had not prepared my son for his first exposure to Little League baseball. His confidence suffered a big blow. I decided then and there that my son would not be in that situation again.

Before the next baseball season started I enlisted the assistance of a baseball instructor at a local facility. When the five lessons began, I asked this coach to go through hitting, throwing, catching, and fielding with my son. I sat back and watched as this skilled coach taught my son. It was fun for me, as a parent, to see his confidence come back as he was able to start hitting the ball and progressing in all other areas of the game. One of the reasons that I wanted Ryan to have outside baseball instruction was to have another adult figure, in addition to me, show confidence in him as an athlete.

When the next season began, Ryan was part of a very good team. The team had a great year and eventually won the state championship. Ryan got a couple of hits and an RBI in the final game. After that victory, as we drove to get a celebration hamburger, he felt a great sense of accomplishment. I was happy as he told me how much he was looking forward to the next baseball season.

If I had not stepped in and done my part, that negative first year could have been the end of competitive baseball and perhaps all sports for my son.

Because of what my son and I did during the off-season, he was able to have a positive baseball experience. He was not the best player on his team, but he was a contributor on a team that won a lot of games. The contrast between his first year, where he felt like a failure, and the second year, where he felt like he was a contributing member of a championship team, was like night and day.

When my second son, Joseph, was old enough to play T-ball I said, "Rather than play T-ball this year, let's you and I go to the park together each week and we'll hit some baseballs. We'll spend an hour there and you'll get the opportunity to hit 100 pitches rather than spending an hour at T-ball and getting to hit three or four times."

As a result of that one-on-one time with my second son, two things happened: first, I got to spend time with my son, and, second, I had many opportunities to build his confidence. With every successful hit, I would verbally pat him on the back and help him believe in himself. This helped prepare him for the time when he will face a real pitcher. When he gets to that point, he'll be much better prepared because he will believe in his skills and his ability to hit a baseball.

OPEN DOORS FOR YOUR CHILD

As your child progresses, you should do all you can to open doors for him to play against opponents who are older and better. That might mean giving your youngster a ride to the gym occasionally. You may have to help him get to know other young athletes and their parents who have similar interests to those of your child. A close friend of mine does this, and helps the coach out at the same time, by providing a schedule and a numerical roster with the telephone numbers of each team member. He gets an opportunity to visit with all the parents as he creates and distributes this document. It's a small thing but it's appreciated by all and can open doors for your child.

If you are knowledgeable in the game and have the time, you could serve as a coach or an assistant coach of a team of players who are a little older than your child. That way he can have the challenge of playing with and against teammates and opponents who are older than he is. It is difficult to ask coaches to provide such opportunities. However, if you know the coaches or are willing to be a coach, those opportunities will be more readily available.

TRAVELING TEAMS

When you feel your son or daughter is ready, one of the important doors that you can open is the door to traveling teams. A traveling team is a team that competes outside of normal elementary, junior high, or high school boundaries. These teams travel out of state and some even out of the country. The purpose of these teams is to allow elite players to compete with and against the best in a particular area away from their home turf. They often can be excellent "playing up" experiences. Another major benefit of these traveling teams is the exposure the athletes receive. College coaches make it a part of their business to know who the up and coming stars are and it is easier for them to go to where the elite are congregated rather than to try to see each young athlete in his or her hometown.

PLAY UP AT CAMPS

Sports camps also offer another terrific opportunity for your son or daughter to play up. At most camps the kids are grouped according to their age. Take the opportunity to talk to the coaches before the camp. If your child is ready to compete with older players, let the coaches know that you would like your child to play in a group above his age group, or two age groups up. You will have to decide where you feel the abilities of your child would be best served.

Be careful with this and always remember that it should be up to your child to want to play up. However, it will be up to you to help facilitate his desire. You can encourage playing up, but ultimately it is up to him. Your future All-American must be his own coach. If he doesn't want to do it, don't force it on him. Playing up certainly can be positive in many ways, but it can also be negative if your child is not ready for it. If you put him in a situation where it is one failure after another with no chance of any success, it is certainly not going to benefit him and he will quickly lose confidence. As younger players compete against older players, the games need to offer a glimpse of some opportunities for success and the hope of more success in time. But if you see that your child is in a situation where he is not getting to experience any success, then it is time to rethink the strategy. It may be best to just encourage your child to play for the fun of it with others at his same level until he develops some confidence in his skills.

PLAY IN LOTS OF GAMES

The key to excellence for your athlete is to have him play and compete in games as much as possible. Your son can play in organized leagues or he can spend time with the gym rats. The benefits are the same. If you want him to become an All-American, open doors for him to play in a multitude of games against players who are better than he is. Do all you can to help him have the opportunity to play a lot—game after game after game and tomorrow the same.

DEVIN DURRANT'S
ALL-AMERICAN PUZZLE

PART 7
LOVE THE GAME

THE FUEL FOR THE ALL-AMERICAN JOURNEY

A love of the game is the fuel needed for the journey to the realm of the All-American. Without a deep love of the game the journey will end far short of the desired destination.

The athlete who loves the game always has time to practice. He seeks out an opportunity to compete just as a hungry person seeks a good meal. He is always able to muster the energy to get to the gym and to go beyond his limits because he loves the game with a passion.

Love has two sons. One is motivation and the other is desire. The athlete who has these powerful fuels burning in him can reach the stars.

WHERE LOVE IS, THERE WILL BE EXCELLENCE

When Larry Bird first excelled in a big way in a high school basketball game, he fell deeply in love with the game. Of that time he said:

The next day's headlines read: BIRD STEALS THE SHOW. That day my life was made. I couldn't believe that it was my name in all the stories and that something I loved to do—and could do well—could make so many people so happy. It was a new and exhilarating experience for me and I decided that day to dedicate myself to being the best basketball player I could possibly be.

From that point on, basketball was all I thought about, all I wanted to do. I couldn't wait for school to let out for the summer so I could play ball. I would play at 6 a.m. before school. I would duck into the gym in between classes to get a few shots up and play again after school into the early hours of the next morning, feeling that sleep was a rude intrusion on my practice time.

Bird explained that later he was tempted to divide his time between two sports:

> Later on, I wanted to resume playing baseball. I wanted to play baseball as a junior and senior, but I never did. By that time I had fallen in love with basketball and when spring came I just couldn't get myself to play baseball. I had to play basketball.[1]

I LOVE BASKETBALL

After my season under the direction of Coach Bolus, I decided to relax and forget basketball for good. Then one day, as I mentioned earlier, a powerful thought swept into my heart: "I love basketball. I want to be a great player." I went outside to shoot and dribble. My love affair with the game had begun and it was a love affair that would bring sweet rewards.

From then on, I loved everything about the game—the bands, the cheerleaders, the rowdy fans—but mostly I just wanted to play. I was thrilled by the competition. I wanted to win. I wanted the respect that comes from being the best.

I wanted our fans to appreciate me and the opposing fans to despise me.

There was nothing that I spent more time doing, other than getting an education, than playing sports. I would play in the cold and snow. I would play in the rain. The weather didn't matter. I loved to play the game.

IS IT LOVE?

Discuss the answers to the following questions with your child:

- Do you dream about your sport during the day?
- Do you seek opportunities to watch and study your favorite player?
- Are you always looking for a game?
- Do you desire to be the first person chosen when choosing up teams?
- Can you feel the chemistry created on a winning team?
- Can you hardly wait until the next game?
- Do you gets goose bumps when you see a championship team celebrate?

If your child answered yes to all these questions, then he loves the game. If there was hesitation in the answers, then maybe a different course for your son would be wise. Excellence is much more attainable if one is doing what he loves to do.

DESIRE IS THE DRIVING FORCE

Some people use the word "motivation" to describe the force that makes a player willing to do what it takes to become an All-American. However, that which will really get your child there is the word "desire." Motivation can come to your son from an outward source such as a coach, a reward, a punishment, or some form of fear. On the other hand, desire comes from your child's heart.

Desire is the driving force that separates the good from the great. I have known players who have had the desire to work hard to be good. They become good and then they rest. They become satisfied. I have known others who have the desire to work hard to be good. They become good and they don't rest. They are never satisfied. Their desire forces them to work even harder to become even greater.

As your child enters the high school and college years of his athletic career, he enters into the most demanding physical, mental, and emotional years of his life. Advise your son that if he thinks he knows what hard work is now, he may have to think again.

If he is going to compete on an All-American level, he will have to be pushed and motivated by others to reach his limits and then, through his internal desire, he will have to push himself beyond those limits as never before. His love of the game will give him the desire to do it.

LIVE THE GAME

When Larry Bird transferred from the University of Indiana to Indiana State he had to sit out a year. He describes how he spent that year:

> It was rough not being able to play in the games, but I played basketball constantly that year. I played more than ever before. In between classes I would go down to the gym and shoot. When they went away on road trips, I played in that gym. The following summer I haunted the Terre Haute Boys' Club. I was always practicing there, always shooting baskets. . . . I'd go home and eat, then come back to the gym and play some more. I mean, I practically lived in that gym.[2]

His choice of how he spent that year led to his becoming an All-American.

As I grew up, I got so I lived to play and to compete. My addiction to the game was the greatest single key to my success as a basketball player. I played in a game as often as I could—one-on-one, two-on-two, five-on-five—it didn't matter. If there was no game to be found, I would work on my shooting or on strength and conditioning. But if I could find a game and play, that was my first choice. A player learns to play the game by playing. Play, play, play.

GREAT SPORTS MOMENTS ARE UNFORGETTABLE

Sports seems to me like a never-ending series of great games and exciting moments. Sports can be enjoyed whether you are a participant or a spectator. However, I believe sports are most enjoyable when shared with a son or daughter.

Pick a day. Any day. Regardless of the day you pick, there is likely to be an interesting sporting event taking place. When you think of your favorite sports moments as a spectator, what comes to mind? For me I see Cal Ripken breaking Lou Gehrig's games-played streak. I see Hank Aaron hitting home run No. 715. I see George Foreman pounding Joe Frazier, and Muhammad Ali whipping Sonny Liston. I see the Red Sox beating the Cardinals in the 2004 World Series to end the "Curse of the Bambino." I see Secretariat winning the first leg of the Triple Crown—I was there in the infield at Churchill Downs. I see Tiger Woods walking up the 18th fairway on his way to his first Masters win with an incredible 12-shot lead. I see Kerri Strug's Olympic vault on a sprained ankle to claim the team gold for the United States women's team in 1996. I could go on. Sports can add a rich taste to life.

MY CHILDREN AND THE GAME

It is heaven for me to pick up a football and go out on the back lawn with my two boys. I have Ryan go long with Joseph in coverage. I fade back and throw the football. Ryan catches it on his fingertips and scores as Joseph, having exerted his all, falls to the turf. Joseph jumps up, and he and Ryan come back to me for the next play. And so it goes. I love it.

During her senior year in high school, my daughter, Laura, competed in a cross-country race. My eyes moistened as I observed her stately form and her magnificent stride. Though her stride was graceful, I could see the pain she felt as she pushed herself. When I greeted her after the race, she fell into my arms. She did not win the race, but she gave all she had. Together we wept. I can't remember a time when I have been filled with more pride and satisfaction than after that race while I held my daughter in my arms.

Years ago, I coached the basketball team of my daughter Emily and her 12-year-old friends. We lost our first game by 30 points. The loss wasn't much fun and it humbled the team. Over the next few weeks we worked on the fundamentals of the game. The girls progressed rapidly from not being able to make a lay-up to being able to make one; from not being able to complete a chest pass to a teammate to being able to do so; and from not being able to defend to being able to stay between an opponent and the basket.

Our last game of the season we played the team that had beat us by 30 points in our first game. This time we were the victors. I celebrated the moment with my Emily. Her excitement was a pleasure to see. She, like her dad, loves to win.

It has been satisfying for me to see my children take an interest and then fall in love with a sport. This past year my son Joseph played both soccer and flag football. At mid-season, I saw the light come on in his head as he suddenly and fully sensed his role in the drama of the game. He realized that he loved competing and since then has not been able to get his fill of sports. Recently, he reported to his mother how much he loves to play kick ball with his fellow third graders.

I don't know if there will be sports in heaven, but I sure have found a lot of heaven in sports. Sports can give a dimension to your life that will help bind your family together.

LOVE OF THE GAME STARTS EARLY

When your son is a toddler buy him a ball. Roll it back and forth with him. You know the drill. Then get him a little goal. Help the little one grasp the concept of the ball going into the goal. Cheer him on. Make the game fun and let the love begin. David Beckham, the great British soccer player, got an early start on his soccer career. He said:

> I'm sure Mum could dig it out of the pile: that first video of me in action. There I am, David Robert Joseph Beckham, aged three wearing the new Manchester United uniform Dad had bought me for Christmas, playing soccer in the front room of our house in Chingford.[3]

The love for soccer and for Manchester United never left young Beckham, and he became the star of that storied team.

As your son gets older, take the opportunity to go with him to a game. There is a different feeling about a game when you are near the action rather than watching it on television. Take him to the arena or ballpark and let him experience the sounds, the smells, the tastes, and the sights. Let him sense the excitement of the competition.

I can remember vividly, as a six-year-old, when my father would take me to the old Smith Fieldhouse at Brigham Young University. I could feel something in the air as we entered the building. They had ice cream sandwiches for sale at the concession stand, and my dad would buy me one as we headed to our seats high up in the bleachers. I still remember the emotions I felt in that building as we watched great athletes play. After the game, we would walk behind the bleachers to the track and field area. I remember jumping into the foam-filled high jump pit. Ever since those early childhood days, I have loved sports arenas and sporting events. The years passed and I was recruited to play basketball at BYU. I looked at my other options but BYU had an unfair advantage over the rest—they had entered my heart years earlier when a dad and his son, ice cream in hand, had cheered together for the Cougars.

INCLUDE BASEBALL AS PART OF THE SUMMER VACATION

Last summer, my wife, Julie, and I took our children to the San Francisco Bay area on a family vacation. The thing that my children remember best was going to an Oakland Athletics' baseball game. The action, the hot dogs and popcorn, sitting there together anticipating every pitch, hoping to see a home run. We were in heaven. The day before, we had toured the home of the San Francisco Giants. My kids, especially my two young sons, were in awe as we looked down on that beautiful playing field. Let one of your family songs be "Take Me Out to the Ball Game."

WATCH AND LEARN

When you cannot go to the arena, watch televised games with your child. Watch and study his favorite players. Sit there close to your son and tell him who the players are so he makes a connection with them. When Sammy Sosa and Mark McGwire were in the home run record chase in 1998, I told my boys that I would give each of them a quarter every time either Sosa or McGwire hit one out of the park. Each morning there was a race between my boys to get the newspaper so we could read the sports pages together to see if either Sosa or McGwire had hit a home run. We did a similar thing when Ichiro was chasing the hits needed to set a season record. Through these experiences my boys are identifying with the greatest athletes in the world and learning to take interest in the morning sports pages. I think they also enjoy accumulating those quarters so they have a little spending money.

Teach your youngster while you watch the game. At the arena or on television, pick out a player who loves the game. Say to your son, "Look at number 35. He is the player that I admire." My father used to do that. He would tell us, "I like that player because of the way he conducts himself on the court. Watch him. He never complains to the referee or to the other players on his team. If he makes a mistake he doesn't get down on himself. He loves the game. Be like him when you play." From that time on, I knew that my father valued players who acted with dignity on the court—players who conducted themselves with class.

David Beckham recalls an earlier time when his soccer-loving father taught him to watch certain players:

> During those first years at United, Eric used to make sure we went to every first-team game at Old Trafford. Not just to watch the game but to watch individual players. I'd think back to Dad taking me to Cup Finals when I was a boy. "Never mind the game, David. Just watch Bryan Robson. Watch what he does."[4]

I enjoy watching championship games. I love to see champions compete. Take your child to such games or watch championship contests on television. Let him feel the pressure of the competition. Let him witness the exhilaration of the victors. Make sure and watch the post-game celebration together. The best part of watching the 2004 Boston Red Sox finally win the World Series was to watch their joyous celebration when the final out was made at first base. Celebrations like that thrill me. I remember many times when I was younger and would witness the ecstasy of a championship celebration, I couldn't wait to get out on my court or lawn afterwards and pretend that

I was the one making the winning catch, the winning throw, or the winning shot. When your child has just watched a great contest, he will have that feeling that makes him want to go play simply for the love of the game.

MOTION PICTURES AND BOOKS

I saw the first *Rocky* movie when I was a high school senior. I loved that movie and have watched it many times since. I recall watching the television movie *Brian's Song* about Gale Sayers and Brian Piccolo. Tears came to my eyes. Movies such as *Rudy, Remember the Titans*, all the subsequent *Rocky* movies, *The Natural*, and *Field of Dreams* all motivated me and filled my heart with a love of the game. Recently, I watched the movie *Miracle* with my daughter Laura. I would have loved to have been able to skate for Coach Brooks—and for my country in the Olympics. The preparation and hard work wouldn't have been much fun, but I believe those guys who skated for him would not trade that experience for anything. I remember watching the Pete Maravich movie *Pistol* with my daughter Emily. We talked about that movie for a long time after. There are other such movies that you can bring home to have your child watch. Better yet, watch them together.

Along with inspirational movies, I also read some great sports books. Each book helped fan the flame of the love of the game within me. Search your public library and book stores for books that will help your son build his vision of the type of athlete he wants to be.

LITTLE LEAGUE

When the time is right, enroll your son in the local leagues. Gradually he'll learn the skills. The time will come when he will really start to "get it."

As I mentioned earlier, this past year I watched as my son Joseph played flag football and I could see a light come on for him. He suddenly became a competitor. Instead of hoping a teammate would stop the runner, he would speed over and rip the flag from the runner. When his team had the ball, he begged his coach for the opportunity to be quarterback. He wanted to score. He was on fire with enthusiasm for football.

There comes a time when the love your child has for the game is not what he borrows from you. It is his own personal, inward feeling. It may be faint at first, but it is real. Be very supportive of his love by continuing to do what you can to get him where he needs to be. Arrange Little League experiences, send him to camps, arrange lessons, buy equipment, go to games played by older players, and talk to him about his interest in sports.

ENCOURAGE PRACTICE AND PLAY

The more he plays, the more he will improve, and the more he improves, the more he will love the game. Hopefully, your son has a friend who also has a desire to excel athletically. Be supportive of this friend. Make him a family friend. Alex Montgomery was that friend for me. He and I loved to play the game.

As I mentioned earlier, my church ran a basketball league. I was not yet old enough to play in the league, but my dad made special arrangements so that I could. My parents paid for camps and for gym shoes they really could not afford so that I could progress as an athlete.

I played Little League football, baseball, and basketball. I played and played and played some more. The more I practiced and played, the more the love of game welled up in my heart. For me the game was the highest form of fun—fun because I was winning more than I was losing. We all enjoy doing that which we feel we do well—especially children. The more I won, the more I practiced because I realized that in order to keep winning I needed to continue to improve.

Do whatever you can to provide your son or daughter with opportunities to practice and to play. Your efforts will not only have rewards in sports, but in your relationship with your child.

OVERCOME ALL OBSTACLES

You have heard it said that love is a verb. That means that we show love through our actions.

Your child will begin to show his attachment to sports through his actions by making sacrifices to practice or to play. Some say that sacrifice is giving up something good today to gain something better in the future. When it came to basketball, that was not true for me. I never felt that it was a sacrifice to spend time and energy to develop my game. I enjoyed doing what it took to get better because of my feelings for the game. Doing hard things made my devotion to the game more intense.

If you force your son to make what he considers to be sacrifices to be a good athlete, it will cause him to lose the desire to compete. Any sacrifice must be his idea, not yours.

THE RIGHT MEDICINE

You may have to prime the pump at times. My sister's son is a big ten-year-old. He has obvious potential as a football player, so his parents signed him up for a team. He loved the idea of playing tackle football. He eagerly went to the first practice. It was on a warm fall day. As the practice progressed, he gasped for breath and sweat poured down his forehead. His love of the game faded. He was ready to turn in his pads.

His parents told him he had committed to play and he must keep going. The next practice was at 6:00 a.m. He had worried about it all night and came into his parent's room crying at 5:30. He told them he was not going to go. They told him that he must go. They drove him to the practice as he silently sobbed. The coach greeted him warmly and praised his ability. My nephew made it through the practice. The coach told him how much he meant to the team. My nephew's love of the game returned and he had a great season. He is eager for the next one. Sometimes a little tough encouragement is the right medicine.

When you see that your son is practicing on his own, be sure and praise him. If you feel he is going at it too hard, don't feel sorry for him. If he is outside shooting baskets in a snowstorm or in the rain, don't make him come in. Let him toughen himself up. Let him shovel the snow off the court so he can play. Don't go out and help him shovel. Let him give something to the game. That will strengthen his attachment to the game all the more. Go out with him on a sunny day, but not on a cold one. He needs to endure most of the cold days on his own.

BUILD YOUR RELATIONSHIP THROUGH SPORTS

A by-product of participating in sports with your child is the close relationship that can be built between the two of you. Participate with him in sports activities either actively by competing together or by enjoying sports as a fan.

Run with your children. Shoot baskets with them, golf with them, and play tennis with them. Last year, I went golfing with my brother Mark. He had his two sons, ages four and six, with him. They each had their own set of junior golf clubs. Mark was doing something he loves—golf—and he was doing it with his sons. That is a tough combination to beat.

My dad always said, "The only time my children talk to me is when I am with them." Think about that for a minute. Sports gives you an excellent opportunity to "[be] with them."

Dad tells this story: "My son, Matt, was in junior high and he was struggling with inward feelings of inadequacy. The two us played one-on-one on our home court. I tried to talk to him by asking, 'How did it go at school today.' He didn't answer.

I asked, 'What did you have for school lunch?' He looked at me in disgust. Then I asked, 'How did it go in gym today?' He started to talk. He expressed his feelings that he wanted to look more like an athlete. He felt he was too small. He told me many things that day on the court. I didn't try to tell him what to do. He didn't want answers. He just wanted to talk. The basketball court was the place. As we went back to the house I could tell he felt better."

My dad and I were always closest on our way to a game, at a game, or discussing a game. Our one-on-one games were really our one-on-one time.

As you spend time one-on-one with your boy, help him to understand and love the chemistry created between players on a winning team. Teach him what a "pick and roll" is. Then run a pick and roll and have him come off the pick and shoot the shot and make it. Then run it again and have him hit you as you roll to the basket. He will love the chemistry of two guys who know how to play together. That good sensation and understanding will add to his feelings for the game.

THE BLESSING OF AN OLDER BROTHER

Larry Bird tells the following about his older brother:

> The first time I ever went to see a high school game was when my brother Mark played his last season. That was in 1969 and I was in ninth grade. By that time, I liked to play. I wound up on what we called the B team as a freshman, so I got to go to games and see Mark play. I remember the first time I ever got really emotional at one of those games. It was a real close game and Mark wound up being fouled. He had to make some big free throws. I was so scared we were going to get beat, but we won. There were tears streaming down my face and I remember thinking, "What's wrong with me? This is what I've been

missing my whole life by not going to these games?" I was just so proud that Mark was my brother. One of my fondest memories is that after that big game, Mark was a hero and when we were all riding back to school on the bus, Mark sat right next to me. Everyone wanted Mark to sit next to them, but he came right over next to me. He made me feel so good when he did that.[5]

I, like Bird, know well the feeling of having an older brother who knew how to make a younger brother feel good. My love of the game was aided greatly by my older brother, Matt, who loved the game as much as anyone I have ever known. He was and still is my hero.

WHAT IF THE LOVE IS MISSING?

Does your child feel that it is fun to play the game? Is there excitement in his heart as he heads toward the gym to shoot some shots or to play in a game? If "fun" is on one side of a scale and "drudgery" is on the other side, fun must always outweigh drudgery or your child will lose interest quickly. You as a parent can assess the level of fun he is having. If there seems to be little or no fun in it for him, then you must evaluate what he needs to do. If you are pushing a lot you may need to back off. Give him time off and then see if later he feels he wants to get back into it. If he doesn't, then help him find other interests. Later he might decide, on his own, to become more involved in the game again.

If, in choosing up sides, your child is the last one chosen or the other kids don't want him on their team at all, then he will naturally dislike the game. In the safe environment of home, practice with him on kicking the ball, hitting the ball, or shooting the ball. Make it fun for him. Praise him for the things he does well. Hopefully this will do two things: first, it will decrease the pain he might be feeling, and second, it will help him gain some skills so that he will be able to enjoy some future success. Perhaps the next time your youngster will not be chosen last. He will be moving in the direction towards loving the game. If he keeps at it, pretty soon he will move up the ladder. However, he might still face the pain at school and in the neighborhood of not doing as well as others.

This can be a very sensitive area. As a parent you have to be there for your boy if he is suffering from feelings of inadequacy. In the case of my son Ryan, when he played baseball, he felt like the last guy chosen his first year and was at the back of the pack. However, he had just enough little successes to cause him to want to stay with it. On this year's team he was probably in the middle of the pack. As a "middle of the packer" a child can really enjoy sports.

As a parent, you can make sure that your child is headed in the direction of success. Evaluate your child's feelings about sports. How does your child feel about them? Do you see some of the signs of the love of the game in your child yet? If you do, your task will be much easier.

On the other hand, maybe your child really doesn't enjoy a particular sport. Maybe he continually dreads going to practice. If this feeling persists, expose your child to other sports. If the light does not come on with sports, try another field. Music, art, or science may be what your child loves. Encourage him and see what the future brings. You may have an All-American musician in your home.

NO INTEREST IN SPORTS

In an effort to get his young son Jake interested in sports, my brother Matt signed him up for Little League baseball. In his very first game, as my brother sat in the stands wringing his hands and hoping his son would have a good experience, Jake began shouting at his father from his first base position. "Dad, I have a question," he yelled.

"Son, wait until the inning is over. You need to concentrate on the game."

This satisfied Jake for a minute or so, but then he repeated his request, "Dad, I really need to ask you the question now."

My brother ran over to the first base coaching box, hoping all the time that no grounder would be hit to Jake while he was distracted. When he got there he anxiously said, "Jake, quickly ask me your question and then focus on this batter."

"Okay, Dad," he replied, "How many different kinds of erosion are there? I can think of wind and water erosion, but I can't remember the others."

His distressed father replied, "Son, I promise we will talk about it as long as you want after this game, but for now you have got to concentrate on baseball." Jake grudgingly turned his attention back to the game.

My brother didn't give up trying to get his son interested in sports. He signed him up for football at the conclusion of the baseball season. He eagerly took him to the team party to kick off the season, which was held at the coach's house. As he chatted with another father, my brother noticed that Jake seemed mesmerized by an NFL highlights video tape playing on a big TV. My brother was thrilled that Jake seemed so entranced, because his son had never shown much interest in football or other sports. He excused himself from his conversation with the other father and sat down next to his son. Just after he did, Jake's face lit up and he turned to his dad with real excitement in his voice. "Dad," he shouted, "I've got it."

"What?" my brother replied, equally excited.

"That music they're playing in the background of this video is the theme song from 'Carmen.'"

My brother would have loved for his son to be a great athlete, but Jake wasn't interested. He loved other things. What I have related happened several years ago. Since that time, my nephew Jake has made himself into a talented musical composer and a scholar. He is now on his way to medical school. In achieving what he has, Jake, in his own way and with the help of his mother and father, has interlocked all nine parts of the All-American Puzzle. He has a very bright future ahead of him.

Fathers need to remember it is not how much they want their child to become an All-American that counts, but how much the child wants it. Your dreams are not necessarily his dreams. But if your future All-American does have those dreams, there is no one who can help him achieve them like a parent can.

Some of you probably love sports so much that you find it difficult to understand why your child does not share your feelings. If you discover he really does not want to put his whole heart, or even a part of it into the game, you may hurt. Given time, the pain will subside.

Even if it is difficult for you to understand your child's feelings, support your son in the things that he does desire to pursue and help him use the same principles for achieving success in athletics to excel in his chosen pursuit outside of athletics.

ONE CHILD DOESN'T HAVE TO FOLLOW THE SAME PATH AS ANOTHER

My younger brother was always expected to love and play sports because I had done well. He was a bit of a free spirit and wanted to do his own thing. He liked to play sports but he didn't want to be so competitive. Much to the dismay of my dad, he refused to try out for the high school basketball team. My mother supported my brother's decision. However, at first my dad did not. Finally he got used to the idea.

Later, my brother played in a league that was just for fun. A league with no pressure. My father signed up to be the coach of that team—not to try to lure his son back to competitive sports—but simply to support him in his enjoyment of athletics as simple recreation. As my brother played in that league, my father shouted constant encouragement to him. My brother loved that, and the two of them who had had a strained relationship became the best of friends.

DEVIN DURRANT'S
ALL-AMERICAN PUZZLE

PART 8
MAKE YOUR OWN LUCK

YOUR CHILD'S DESTINY IS IN HIS OWN HANDS

I believe that you and I determine our own destiny. I agree with the great Roman poet, Virgil, who said, "Fortune favors the bold."

An observer might say to an athlete who made All-American, "You sure have been lucky in your life."

The athlete could reply, "Yes, I have been. But most of the luck was the result of things that I did." The athlete might also say, "The harder I worked, the luckier I seemed to get."

An observer might also say to a puzzle assembler, "You are so lucky all those pieces came together to make that beautiful scene."

The puzzle builder could reply, "Those pieces did not come together. I brought them together piece by piece and part by part. Over and over again. Thousands of times. And through it all, not one piece came together by luck."

AN ATHLETE HAS TO MAKE HIS OWN LUCK

If an athlete puts all his might, mind, and strength into interlocking all the pieces of every part of his All-American Puzzle he will, when success comes, look back and be amazed at all the so-called "lucky breaks" he got along the way. On the other hand, if an athlete ignores some of the parts of his puzzle and only relies on the physical gifts he inherited and the people and circumstances he hopes will favor him along the way, he will, after falling short, look back and wonder why lady luck never shined on him.

Our common goal is to help our children become All-Americans—successful on and off the field of competition. Whether or not that happens is not a matter of luck. It is not because of someone else. Success happens because you and your child make it happen.

NOT UNLUCKY BUT UNWISE

If a young athlete does not reach his desired goals it is partly due to the fact that sometime during his career he made some decisions that were not bold. He stepped back when he should have stepped forward. He was negative when he should have been positive. He missed some opportunities that came his way. He did not capitalize on some key relationships. He stayed away when he should have followed up. He didn't build trust and friendship when he could have.

I guess you could say that having a good coach makes a young athlete lucky. However, what makes the time with that coach valuable is that the young person is coachable.

It is lucky to be tall. However, what makes height an advantage is that your child works hard to learn the moves that make a tall player effective.

It is lucky to play in front of a scout who can extol your

young athlete's virtues as a player. However, what makes the meeting important is that your child has developed the ability to impress the scout.

It is lucky to be on a good team. But what makes the experience meaningful is that your youngster did what it took to make the starting five.

It is lucky for your child to be in a position to take a last second shot to win a game. But what makes the opportunity a joy is that he prepared for the moment by making thousands of shots in practice so that he could make the big shot in the game.

It is lucky to be in the right place at the right time. However, what makes the timing significant is that your child brought with him the ability that was needed at that right place and at that right time.

So we see that luck is not determined by circumstances, rather it is determined by your child.

No matter how old your child is now, or what team he wants to make, or how much playing time he desires to have, don't ever blame your child's lack of success on somebody else or on bad luck. His success is in his hands.

THE RIGHT COMBINATION

I was lucky to grow up in a family that encouraged me to participate in sports and helped me to develop a desire to be a good athlete. However, it was up to me to love the game and to work at it.

As a young boy, I read books about a variety of athletes. The first one I remember reading was about Babe Ruth. Later I read about Walt Frazier, Earl "The Pearl" Monroe, Connie Hawkins, Muhammad Ali, Julius Erving, Rick Barry, and others. I also watched great athletes compete on television. Through my reading and watching I gained a desire and a dream to be an athlete.

I had just the right coaches for me. They were the right coaches for me because I wanted them to be and I allowed them to be.

My Little League baseball coach, Don Grayson, encouraged me and helped me gain confidence. He taught me the fundamentals of baseball and introduced me to organized competition. But it was up to me to compete for him.

My Little League football coaches motivated me and introduced me to physical contact. I loved my days as a young football player.

I've mentioned my church coach, Steve White. I did what he asked me to do. He was very good to me. He was a friend to Rick Bolus. He told Coach Bolus about me and gave me a positive recommendation. Without Steve White's help, Coach Bolus may have cut me from his team. However, I was the one who did everything possible to impress Steve White. If he had not liked the way I played for him, he wouldn't have recommended me to his friend. Things work like that. It is what you do that makes it happen.

In junior high I was coached by the perfect coach for me at that time in my life—Coach Bolus. He made me a better player because I was coachable. It was not luck that made him so important to me. It was I who was willing to be molded.

Then Jim Spencer became my high school coach. He instilled in me the desire to be a champion. I was like a sponge to all he taught. I made the most of everything he said.

For three years I had the good fortune of being coached by Frank Arnold, who had been an assistant to John Wooden at UCLA. He was accustomed to winning and he built a winning culture at BYU. He demanded excellence in every detail. I gave him my all and he rewarded me with great opportunities.

Ladell Andersen became my coach for my senior year of college. He had been a successful college coach and had also been a successful coach at the professional level in the old ABA. His system allowed me to be a star. I took advantage of that and with the help of some very unselfish teammates made All-American.

THE RIGHT TIMING

One day several years ago, a close friend and I were discussing how each of us had benefitted in our pasts from excellent timing. Because of our fortunate timing, we decided to give ourselves some nicknames. My friend was dubbed "Rolex" (he had a lot more money than I did) and I was designated "Timex." We had a good laugh over our "timing" nicknames. Since that time I have reflected a lot on the importance of good timing. It is a very serious matter and one that will have a big impact on your son or daughter's success.

The timing that unlocked so many doors for me in my basketball career began in elementary school. As I mentioned earlier, as a third grader, my teachers, the school principal, and my parents all concurred that I should be moved up from the third grade to the fourth grade in the middle of the school year. This mid-year promotion made all the difference in my life. It set off a chain reaction of timing that had an impact on me every year thereafter.

However, even though the timing was right for me from that point forward, that was not as important as the fact that I was ready to make the most of the timing.

Because of moving up a grade, I was later in the eighth grade when I should have been in the seventh grade. Because of that promotion, I was able to play under Coach Bolus. The next year he left coaching and moved on to another position. If he had not been my coach that year, I would not have received those vital pieces of my puzzle that he gave me. My future in basketball would have suffered and I would not have become an All-American. However, if I had not been ready and willing when I was under his direction, it could have been a negative rather than a positive experience.

Because of excellent timing I was able to start, as a junior, at Provo High with four seniors who all went on to play at the college level. Those older teammates taught me a lot. If I had only been a sophomore that year, I probably would not have had that experience. The next year, my senior year in high school, I was a starter with a new group of very unselfish teammates— Ed Terris, Dave Asay, Eugene Paulsen, and Dave Collins. The experiences I had during both my junior and senior year were positive because of my respect for my older teammates during my junior year and later because of my love for my teammates during my senior year. If I had had a different outlook toward either of these two sets of teammates, my high school basketball experience could have been much less productive.

Again "my one year ahead" timing made it so I was able to begin my college career by playing for two years at BYU with Fred Roberts, Greg Kite, and Danny Ainge. Each of these men went on to long and successful careers in the NBA. If I had not been a college freshman until a year later, I would not have had that two-year opportunity to learn from each of these terrific players. But if I had not been receptive to their examples and leadership I would not have profited from being their teammate.

The best decision I made in my life up to that point was after my sophomore year of college when I decided to interrupt my basketball career to serve a two-year mission for The Church of Jesus Christ of Latter-day Saints. I had no idea what the results would be from putting my athletic career on hold for two years. However, the results of that decision helped me to put together the final pieces of my All-American Puzzle.

That two-year delay in my athletic timing changed the makeup of the BYU team. I had loved competing with my pre-mission teammates. But when I returned from my mission most of them had moved on. My "new" team needed a leader. In that situation I was called on to be more of a scorer and this put me in the national limelight. This turned out to be good fortune for me because I was ready to be a leader and to do whatever it took to help the team win. At that time the team needed me to be a scorer.

Without the two-year delay I would never have had the opportunity to play for Coach Ladell Andersen. Just before my senior season he became my coach. He was accustomed to a "star system" and allowed me to play the entire game. He ran the offense through me, which gave me many opportunities to display my skills. His philosophy allowed me to get considerable national attention. He gave me the green light, but it was up to me to get it done.

What I am saying is that every situation in my life— including the people and the timing—had to be just right for me to succeed. However, it was up to me, as it is for your child, to deliver—to interlock each piece of the puzzle.

BE READY FOR THE OPPORTUNITY

You will find in your child's life he will meet people who will be able to aid him in his quest for excellence. Help your youngster watch for these people and cultivate their trust and friendship. Do your part to help your child maximize each relationship, each coach, and each situation that he meets. On the other hand, he could meet a coach who could really help, but you or he has an attitude that won't allow the coach to help. Don't blame a coach for your child's lack of success. Maybe the timing was right for him to be your child's coach but your child was not ready to learn. He was not willing to do what the coach asked of him. A young player can be presented with a lot of good opportunities, but he needs to be willing and able to move though the doors when they open.

BE WILLING TO KNOCK
ON OTHER DOORS

If your son feels unlucky because one door closes for him, then help him make his own luck by knocking on a nearby door that is ready to open. I read an example of this in an article written by Dick Harmon in the *Deseret News* on August 19, 2003. He describes the career of a football player named Brandon Stephens.

In high school, Brandon was a *Parade* All-American tight end. As a freshman at Brigham Young University he suffered a season-ending knee injury. After a two-year LDS Church mission, he felt his best chance for playing time was to become a defensive end. His coaches, however, felt his talent was more suited to being a pass-protecting, run-blocking, offensive tackle. Of Stephens, Harmon wrote, "Now a senior, Stephens has experienced being converted, refitted, spun around, transitioned, reinvented, relabeled, and reprocessed during his BYU career."

In the article, former BYU coach Gary Crowton said this about Stephens: "I never saw him play tight end, but I think he should have been an offensive tackle all along. As a defensive tackle, he was too tall and they could get to his legs. He's athletic enough to play defensive end, but offensive tackle is his spot."

Of his career thus far, Stephens said, "Many people could be bitter over this situation. Others take a situation like this and see it as an opportunity. I see it as chance and I really feel right at home, where I belong."

Some opportunities will come without much effort. Others you and your child will have to seek as Brandon Stephens did. If one door doesn't open, knock on another one. If your child is ready, good things will happen to him.

YOU CAN SEE THE WHOLE PICTURE

As you look back on your past, you can probably recall relationships with people and experiences that have profoundly influenced the course of your life. Yet, when you were in the midst of these experiences, people, and events, you may not have recognized the impact they would have on your future.

Your child, right now, is in the midst of the people and experiences that will determine the success or non-success of his chosen pursuit. From your son's present vantage point, it will be hard for him to put these things into proper perspective. From your broader view, seen from your extra years and experience, you can more fully understand what is happening. You are in a position to help your child wisely progress to where he wants to be.

At these critical times, your son may not recognize when he is missing the boat of opportunity. It is up to you to keep your eyes open and help your son get the most out of each relationship and every experience. Help him make his own luck.

HELP YOUR CHILD BUILD RELATIONSHIPS

You can open doors for your athlete that can lead to some key relationships. You can choose to have your son play for a particular coach. You can put him in a situation where opportunities to make the team and get playing time will be more likely. Ask yourself the question, "Is my child going to have an opportunity to play and is he going to play for someone who I think can best help him progress?" If the answer is no, then, if your child agrees, do what you can to change things.

You might steer your youngster to a particular school, or to a particular coach. You may not know whether or not you made the right decision until years later. All you can do is make the best decision with the information that you have today, and then once you have made your decision do all you can to make it the right one.

THE SCHOOL TIMING DECISION

One of the questions many athletic-minded parents have is, "When should I start my child in elementary school?" It may be an advantage to start him or her a year later than the others his age. That way, instead of being a 17-year-old senior in high school, he will be an 18-year-old senior in high school. That extra year of physical maturity could make a lot of difference on the field of athletic competition. Some feel that the best course of action is to hold a child back a year to give him an advantage later. In my case the opposite was true when I was advanced to the fourth grade halfway through my third-grade year. That advancement was the best thing that could have happened to me because, in later years, the key coaches and opportunities in my life would not have been there if I had come along a year later. It's very difficult to know whether to move a boy up a grade or hold him back a grade, or let just him stay with his normal class. That last option seems the most reasonable to me.

Be aware of what is happening in your child's life. Change the things you can change and help your child make the best of what can't be changed. Be reasonable. Always remember that the lessons learned from athletic competition are far more important than the trophies that may or may not end up on a shelf in your home.

DEALING WITH INJURIES

One area of athletic life that you cannot control is the injuries that occur during competition. If your son competes athletically, over the span of 10 or 15 years, the likelihood is extremely high that he will be injured along the way. The severity of the injury might mean that your athlete's sports career is over, or he might be able to heal and come back.

At the beginning of my senior year of high school, I struggled with back spasms. With the help of "Marvelous Marv," the pain subsided to the point that it was bearable enough for me to play. The good luck in that injury was in its timing. It happened early in the season. I could have had that same problem right before the state tournament. If that had been the case, I may not have been able to play in critical games leading up to and including the state tournament, where my team won the state championship. As a result of that success, doors opened to national all-star games and a college scholarship.

My second injury occurred just before my sophomore year in college. At that time, I broke my ankle—bad luck. Again the good luck was in the timing. It happened during the pre-season and I had the opportunity to heal and come back and play in the opening game of the season. With my injuries, I was unlucky because I suffered the injury and yet lucky because of the timing of the injury.

However, another guy on my team was not so lucky. I mentioned him earlier. His name was Mike Maxwell. Mike was destined to become an All-American. Unfortunately, he blew out his knee so severely that, although he recovered from his injury, he was never again able to perform as he had before. Now, years later, he is a very successful high school coach. He has done things in other areas of his life that are much more important than being an All-American in sports. Maybe his injury was not as unlucky as it seemed.

To go through athletics without a career-threatening or career-ending injury is a great blessing. If your athlete does get injured, you can do more to help him maintain his perspective than can any other person.

DEALING WITH JEALOUSIES

One of the challenges that you and your athletically successful child will face along the way might be jealous teammates or their parents. The other parents may not appreciate your child's success. Each parent wants his or her child to be in the limelight and to be the star. Have understanding for them, and help your child move beyond the jealousies. Fortunately for me, the parents of my teammates through the years were supportive when I received individual recognition. I think the main reason for that was because we were successful as a team. Nevertheless, beware of jealousies. You may feel them towards others or you may be the target of them.

On the All-American road are many obstacles. Overcoming each obstacle can be an exciting adventure and if handled well, each experience will help your son in his quest to make his own luck.

THE DREAM

BE YOUR OWN COACH

BE COACHABLE

WORK WORK WORK

RODEO TOUGH

DARE MIGHTY THINGS

LOVE THE GAME

MAKE YOUR OWN LUCK

GIFTS FROM GOD

DEVIN DURRANT'S
ALL-AMERICAN PUZZLE

PART 9
GIFTS FROM GOD

NO EFFORT REQUIRED

We have now discussed the first eight parts of the All-American Puzzle. Your child and all other young athletes can be equal as they work to assemble all the pieces that make up the first eight parts of the All-American Puzzle. However, there are other qualities and blessings that an athlete receives through no effort of his own. They come to him as, what I call, gifts from God.

HARD WORK ISN'T ENOUGH

There is a myth that we hear many times in our society that says, "You can achieve anything you want if you work hard enough." There may be some truth to that saying in some areas of life, but the saying doesn't work in athletics. Without the right set of gifts from God, there is no way your child can become an All-American. If your young aspiring athlete is short and slow, even if he successfully interlocks all the other eight pieces of the All-American Puzzle, there is still no way he can become

179

the best of the best. To say otherwise would be an untruth. I have seen a lot of guys who worked hard at sports, but who were not blessed with certain gifts from God and were never as successful as they longed to be.

Each sport and each position in that sport requires certain physical attributes. If your child has these attributes, he will have an advantage over the less gifted in that position in that sport. It cannot be changed with all the hard work in the world.

SOME "TOO LATE" ADVICE

Tall kids come from tall parents. So if you want to raise an All-American basketball player, it would help the process for you to marry a tall spouse. However, it is not mandatory. There are anomalies. An anomaly is something that happens that defies the natural order. If you are short and your spouse is short and you dream of raising a tall basketball player, then you better do some hoping and praying for an anomaly. However, while height is helpful for excelling in the sport of basketball, there are other physical attributes needed to excel that are not so obvious. One such trait is speed. So, if you're not yet married, challenge your girlfriend to a 100 meter race. If she beats you, move forward to marriage. Or if your sweetheart is a marathon runner, then slip a ring on her finger because endurance is a big plus in basketball, and in other sports.

CONTROL WHAT YOU CAN

Apart from your choice of a marriage partner, your child's physical attributes are out of your control. Oh sure, you can feed him double thick milkshakes and have him lift weights and thus add a few pounds and some muscle. But beyond that your child is what he is.

So, what do you do if your youngster doesn't have a full set of the gifts from God required to be a great athlete? That is what this book is about. You can't control your youngster's growth or speed, but there are things that you can help him control. These things are not matters of the body, they are matters of the heart. The other eight parts of the All-American Puzzle are the controllable variables of athletic excellence.

ASSESSING YOUR CHILD'S GIFTS FROM GOD

Take a close look at the physical attributes your son or daughter has. Different sports have differing sets of physical requirements that would make an athlete "a natural" in a particular sport. As parents, you will want to guide your maturing child to a sport and a position in that sport in which his physical attributes would most likely bring success.

For now let's consider this matter of physical attributes as it relates to basketball. What makes a young person a natural in the sport of basketball?

Extra height is always helpful. With some young children it is easy to see that they will be tall. However, in many children, it isn't until he or she begins to mature that physical traits become obvious. So don't be too quick to decide what physical attributes your child will have at maturity. Look at your son now and ask, has he been blessed by God with any or all of the following gifts?

- Extra height
- Lightning speed
- Tremendous jumping ability
- Quick feet
- Large hands
- Great court vision
- Broad shoulders
- Untiring endurance

A few young basketball players have a complete set of these physical attributes. If that is the case with your son then the future is bright. He could indeed become an All-American. However, even with a few of the gifts listed above missing from your child's gift set, he could still become a highly successful athlete in the sport of his choice. Your child doesn't need all the gifts; he just needs enough of the right gifts to excel in his chosen sport. This book is important for the parent of the child with all the gifts but it is much more important for the parent of the child that may be missing a gift or two from the set.

MY GIFTS

I was blessed by God with certain gifts. I was moderately tall at six-foot seven-inches. My body was not that of a body builder, but I was not skinny. I weighed about 200 pounds in college. I was endowed with superior endurance. I had a natural gift to make moves that allowed me to get inside shots. I was not amazingly fast, but I could get down the court better than most on the break. I did not have large hands. However, I could catch the ball well. I could jump, but not out of the gym like some teammates of mine.

I was tall enough, agile enough, and quick enough to get my shot off over good defenders, and I was a better than average jumper with good timing. While I wished I could have jumped higher, I still had some fun moments when dunking the ball. We had a play at BYU that caused the fans to go wild. When we had the ball out of bounds under our basket, Fred Roberts would throw it in. I would stand at the end of the foul line directly in front of Fred. Usually the other team would be in a zone defense. I would break through the two outer defenders and come hard to the basket. Fred would throw it up near the rim and I would jump up, catch the basketball, and dunk it as hard as I could. I loved to jump and make that play. It was a fun payday for all the torturous jumping exercises I used to do.

I could run long distances with ease because of my endurance. As a game progressed, I would not get very tired.

This gave me a great advantage over my opponents. It made it so that I could play a lot of minutes without needing a break. Coach Andersen, my coach during my senior year at BYU, told me I could stay in the game until I felt too tired to be effective. Early in the year I took myself out of one game because I felt tired. After sitting for a minute, I said to myself, "I don't like sitting on the bench and I'm not that tired, " so I asked him to put me back in. After that I played almost every minute of every game my senior year. My endurance was a key piece of my All-American Puzzle.

STAND TALL

One of your joys as a father of a young child will be to watch him or her grow. In our house we had a doorway where my father would have me stand, shoeless, against the door jamb. He would tell me, "Stand as tall as you can." He would then put a book on my head. When the book was level he would make a mark with a pencil. He would write the date by the measurement.

Often, the new mark was right where the old one was. Then there would come times when the mark was a little higher. If I had grown, my dad would get excited and so would I. We could record my height, but we had no control over it. The amount of growth was a gift from God.

You may notice your son is faster or quicker than others. Observe his endurance during vigorous activities. You will, as do most dads, see exceptional gifts in your son. However, there will come times when you will have to be objective as you assess your son's overall set of physical attributes, attributes which will give him the opportunity to be a great athlete, or the lack of such attributes, which will limit, though not eliminate his chances for future success in athletics. You will then need to be his counselor and consoler as he struggles when he compares himself to others with a more obvious set of athletic gifts.

If you and I were having a heart-to-heart talk about your young athlete's physical gifts, what would you tell me?

How do you feel that he compares to others in the physical characteristics we have described? Is he a tall, quick, leaping, broad-shouldered physical specimen? A phenom who has the potential to dominate in basketball? Or is he, in your opinion, one of the least gifted? Most likely your child will be somewhere in between.

When you evaluate your young player's God-given physical gifts, look at the total package of attributes. While he may not have a complete set of physical gifts, he may have a very positive overall combination. That was the case for me.

As I said, I was not really tall by basketball standards, but I was tall enough. I was not fast compared to the speedsters of my day, but I was fast enough. I was not able to jump as if I was on a trampoline, but I could jump pretty well. I had great lung capacity—better than most. I had good peripheral vision. All in all, although I was not blessed with one amazing athletic gift, I had an excellent overall package of gifts.

GIFTS CAN COME LATER

Don't feel that your child's junior high lack of size, speed, and jumping ability will not change. They might. Of Michael Jordan it was said:

> As far as basketball, Mike was just another gunner as a ten- and eleven-year-old. He'd take thirty shots a game and if you passed him the ball, it wasn't coming back. In the ninth grade, he was just a 5'9" guard, that's all. Don't let anyone tell you they saw greatness back in those days.[1]

Remember, as time goes by, your youngster might grow. He might get faster. He might really fill out. He might still become a great jumper. His hands might grow. He may come into his body and become more coordinated. A year or two of physical development can make all the difference.

COURSE CORRECTIONS

If your young one doesn't have a good collection of basketball-related gifts then perhaps he is best suited for a different sport. Help your child reflect upon the gifts that he has been blessed with. Help him choose a sport that fits his natural gifts.

Even if it appears your son is not going to be tall, lightning quick, or an incredible jumper, he can still choose basketball. Your son may have a love of basketball that can cause him to feel that it is the game for him even though he is not a natural in that sport. If he chooses basketball, he can still receive many rewards for his efforts, among them the thrill of being a member of a team and enjoying the camaraderie with the other players. He may also be rewarded by getting some key minutes in front of the crowd, maybe even the chance to make a vital contribution to the team's overall success. A player certainly doesn't have to be an All-American to make a contribution to the team and to enjoy the satisfaction of athletic success.

I recall one young man in the movie *Hoosiers*. He was a substitute who obviously had been given very few of the basketball gifts from God. However, he had a deep love for the game. He was the player in the district championship game who had to go in at the end of a dramatically close contest. Shortly after he entered the game, he was fouled. In order for his team to win he had to make two foul shots. He stepped up to the line and did it. He and his team were winners. No one on the team was as thrilled as he was. Unexpectedly, he had made a major contribution to his team's success.

WHAT ABOUT THE HEART?

Although certain inherited physical attributes are major factors in an athlete's potential to become an All-American, there are inward qualities that are not genetic. These intangibles greatly influence an athlete's potential to excel. These inward, unseen qualities make up what are often referred to as the "heart of a champion."

Good coaches will recognize this important attribute. In one situation, the former players of a long-time high school coach advised him that they were going to honor him at an upcoming banquet. They asked him which of all the hundreds of former players he wanted to deliver the main speech. The coach paused and thought. Then he spoke a player's name. He added, "He was a player who had no size, no speed, and no natural ability. But he had a heart that made him great."

These inward qualities of a champion are:
- Dreams of greatness.
- Coaches himself during all the unsupervised minutes and hours of every day.
- Does whatever the coach asks him to do.
- Works, works, and works some more.
- Is mentally and physically tough.
- Confidently dares to do mighty things.
- Loves the game.
- Makes his own luck.

Does that list sound familiar? That is right. It is a list of the eight parts of the All-American Puzzle which are in your hands. These parts are the matters of the heart and mind. They are the controllable variables of athletics and life.

NATURE OR NURTURE

These inward qualities or traits, unlike physical gifts, don't come from the youngster's family tree. They come from somewhere within the individual. It seems to me that they can be nourished from scratch in any boy or girl who is willing to seek and develop them. These inward qualities have their seeds in the mental, emotional, and spiritual part of the young person.

These inward traits can complement the physical attributes of the gifted, and can also elevate the physical ability of the less physically gifted.

THE STRENGTH OR WEAKNESS OF THE HEART

While I was a high school senior, I played in three different McDonald's All-American games as a member of the United States team. In Washington, D.C., we played against an all-star team from that area. While in Philadelphia, Pennsylvania, we played against the best of that area. And in Louisville, Kentucky, we played against the Kentucky-Indiana All-Stars. The teams were made up of the best players from around the United States and the best from the geographic areas I have mentioned. In those three games, I probably played with and against 50 different guys who were considered the best high school seniors in the country at that time. The talent level was very impressive.

I remember my first All-American game in Washington, D.C. The first practice was held at DeMatha High School. I don't think I have ever felt as intimidated as I felt during that practice. I was on the same court with a guy named Cornelius Thompson, who was about six-foot-eight, 260 pounds; and Mark Aguirre, another very physically mature and strong high schooler, who went on to a successful NBA career. They both seemed so big. I felt very out of place because I wasn't as big as these other guys were, not even close. Other players were lightning fast, which was also very intimidating.

But over time, by competing in these three All-Star games, I realized there were a lot of things that were more important than physical size and speed in becoming a successful basketball player. I began to see that a major component of success came from within. I went from feeling out of place during that first practice because of my skinny frame to feeling like I belonged.

Eventually, I was able to lead my team to victory in the last All-Star game, the Derby Festival Basketball Classic, and be named the Most Valuable Player because I used some of the inward traits that I had developed.

THE NEGLECTED FARM

It's like the story of the man who took over a run-down but fertile farm. After two years of back-breaking work, the farm was productive and beautiful. The local minister came by and looking at the glorious sight said, "It's amazing what you and the Lord have done with this farm." The farmer replied, "Yes indeed. But you should have seen it when the Lord had it all by himself."

When a young person doesn't work to develop the gifts the Lord has given him, he will be no more productive than the neglected farm.

During the three high school All-American games, I played with many guys who had been blessed with amazing physical gifts from God. Some were tall and strong physical specimens. Others were amazingly fast. Some could jump so high it appeared they could fly. But the most remarkable thing to me was that most of them were not successful in college basketball and were not drafted into the NBA. They failed to fully develop what they had been given at birth.

YOU CAN CATCH UP

If you are reading this book and your child is a high school senior, you may still feel like your son has not yet reached his full athletic potential. Just because an athlete does not make an All-American team in high school does not mean that he won't make an All-American team in college. Many times players who have success early in life sit back and think they have it made. Athletic superiority comes to them so easily from ninth to twelfth grade because of their physical gifts that they think it will be just as easy for them as freshmen in college. They do not develop some of the essential inward traits, and in time, they are passed up by other players. Why are they passed up? Because they failed to interlock all the parts of their All-American Puzzle.

All avid sports fans can list players who were obviously endowed with the natural gifts that are needed to become an All-American, but who lacked the gift of hustle, the gift of giving their all, and more. One of the saddest occurrences in sports is when a gifted player fails because of lack of effort. On the other hand, one of the most joyous occurrences in sports is to see a less-gifted player take what he has been given by God and make the absolute most of it.

THE GREATEST GIFT OF ALL—FAMILY

Another gift that we have no control over is the gift of a family—brothers and sisters, parents, grandparents, great-grandparents, etc. The family is the key to success in life. It's a wonderful gift when you can count on a member of your family to be there physically or in spirit when you need them. Paul O'Neill of the New York Yankees said:

> And then, at my lowest low, an envelope arrived in the mail, addressed to me in my father's handwriting. As I sat down to read it, I unfolded a long letter that he'd written by hand on lined yellow paper. This was one of the few times Dad had ever put his feelings to paper for me. He recounted our family history, how his father had played in the minors and his uncle had played in the Pioneer League, and how he himself had played baseball. Reading his words off the page, it was almost as if he was physically there putting his arm around me, energizing me with the will to carry on, continuing with his pep talk about how I was his son and I was not going to quit.
>
> When I put the letter away, a subtle shift had taken

place inside, giving me a sense of certainty that this was not the end of my baseball ride. I resolved to give it one more go, for the sake of myself and for the family. That letter propelled me to [break] out of my slump.[2]

When your athlete is young your family is a positive voice that tells him who he is and what he stands for. Perhaps this family voice that speaks to his heart comes from both of his parents or from one of them, or maybe it comes from a grandparent, or from an uncle or an aunt or from an older brother or sister. You must create such a voice within your young son or daughter.

This family voice, which will be deep inside your child's heart, will speak to him when he needs it most. It will give him the power to keep going when it seems he has already given his all. It will help him turn away from the negative influences that could destroy his ability to be his best. This voice will make him want to make his family proud that he is one of them.

Some of the negative voices of this world will also speak to your child. When the world's voice conflicts with the family voice, encourage your child to turn his back on the world and follow the family voice.

There is something else that is vitally important to your youngster's All-American quest. Of all the coaches, all the opportunities, and all the other factors in your child's success, none will be as important as will his good fortune to be part of your family.

Having a strong, supportive family will give him an inner peace that will enable him to have that extra something that will allow him to overcome all odds and take him all the way to his dream.

PARENTS

Pat Riley in his book, *The Winner Within*, tells of an experience that took place during the NBA playoffs between the Los Angeles Lakers and the Boston Celtics in 1985. The Lakers had lost in the finals the year before to the Celtics. After the loss the players were accused by the press and the fans of being "chokers." Some referred to them as the Los Angeles "Fakers."

The Lakers players and coaches were determined that the results would be different in 1986. However, in the first game of this series, they were humiliated by the Celtics 148 to 114.

All the players had given a lackluster performance, but the one factor that seemed to be the main cause of the defeat was the sub-par performance of the all-time-great, Kareem Abdul-Jabbar.

Three days later, it was time for the second game. The coaches and all the players arrived at the bus to go from the hotel to the arena early except for Kareem. Finally at a half minute to six, Kareem came running up with his father.

Coach Riley could hear Kareem and his father talking to each other on the bus all the way to the arena. He then knew what he should say in his pre-game talk.

Of that talk Riley recalled:

> I faced Kareem directly and said, . . . When I saw you and your father on the bus today, it made me realize what this whole moment is about. . . . Maybe you needed that voice. Maybe each and every one of us in this room needs to hear that kind of a voice right now, the voice of your dad, the voice of a teacher, the voice of somebody in the past who was there when you didn't think you could get the job done.

Coach Riley recalled for the players how, when he was a young boy, his father instructed his older brothers to make him play each day against older guys who devastated him. How he hid in the garage crying after such defeats. How his father came there and carried him into the house. Back inside he told the older brothers to take young Pat back the next day to play against those great and painful odds. Riley quoted his father, saying:

> "I want you to take him down there because I want you to teach him not to be afraid. That there should be no fear. Teach him that competition brings out the very best and the very worst in us. Right now it's bringing out the worst, but if he sticks with it, it's going to bring out the best." He then looked at his eight-year-old, teary-eyed son and said, "Pat, you have to go back there."

Coach Riley then shared another quote from his father. These words came in 1970 as his father and mother were leaving Pat's wedding reception. Pat, at the time was in the midst of a very challenging time in his basketball career. His father counseled him, saying:

> "Just remember what I taught you. There will come a time. And when that time comes, you go out there and kick somebody's ass. This is that time, Pat."

Coach Riley told his team that those were the last words he ever heard his father say. His father died not long after that. Coach Riley continued with his own words:

> Every now and then there comes a day someplace, sometime, you simply have to plant your feet, stand firm and make a point about who you are and what you believe in. . . .
>
> It was [my father's] message that I gave the Lakers that day. It came from the heart. It was inspired by Kareem Abdul-Jabbar and his father and how they connected with each other.[3]

All the Lakers listened intently. They then went out and soundly defeated the Celtics that night. Kareem had 37 points, 18 rebounds, and six blocked shots.

There is a voice within your son that speaks to him from the relationships he has within his family. That voice within him will strengthen him and lift him throughout his life, particularly when times get tough. It is not a voice pleading for luck. It is a voice pleading for an honest effort.

My mother's voice has always been with me. Whenever I would leave home to go play a game, she would always say, "Now don't you forget to shoot tonight." During my high school and college games, she could often be heard during the game shouting, "Kill 'em." All was right in the world when I was able to look over and see my Mom in the stands cheering me on. But the words of my mother that I hear now in my mind are, "I love you and I'm proud of you."

GRANDPARENTS

Charles Barkley writes, with regret, that as he grew up there was no father in his home. However, he was blessed with an extremely supportive mother and wonderful grandparents. Charles writes with gratitude for his grandfathers:

> My grandfathers were spectacular. I was probably too immature to understand at the time how necessary they were to a kid's success. It's just so difficult to be successful without that kind of support network.

However, the most influential voice in Barkley's life was his no-nonsense grandmother. She kept him in check by not permitting him to have a "big-man-on-campus" attitude. He said:

> My grandmother has always been the rock of the family. She's really strong, assertive, aggressive. I've always been just like my grandmother, stubborn and strong-willed. I'm 100 percent like her. My grandmother was the

father-figure in our family since my father wasn't there.
She took charge of all the important situations, made
the difficult decisions. She handled all the discipline. . .
Whatever grandma said, that was it. It wasn't up for a
vote. There was no debate.[4]

Charles Barkley's heart was strengthened by the strong
family voice inside him.

BROTHERS AND SISTERS

A profoundly important voice in my life was my older
brother, Matt. I always wanted to do well because I knew he
believed in me and I never wanted to let him down. He had
a desire to be a great athlete but he wasn't blessed with some
of the physical gifts I received. He could have made my life
miserable when success came my way. He did just the opposite.
He was more excited than I was with every accomplishment in
my life. My gratitude to him for his goodness to me over the
years cannot be adequately expressed.

If you have two sons, I am going to bet the younger one will
enjoy more athletic success than the older one. We've already
mentioned the impact Larry Bird's older brother had on him.
I am sure there are a number of All-Americans out there who
have an older brother to thank for their success. I do. His voice
lifted me on many occasions.

CONCLUSION

No blessing is greater than a supportive, strong family.
Without that part of the All-American Puzzle, the other parts
won't matter nearly as much.

As I look back, I remember the positive words of my parents,
my siblings, my Aunt Sharoni, my grandmas, my teachers, my
leaders, my coaches, and others in the community. It is the
relationships I have had with these people that have put into
my heart a desire to excel—to excel not only athletically, but in

all areas of my life. Give your child a positive inward voice that can only come from the family.

May your child successfully interlock every piece of every part of the All-American Puzzle and may excellence be a part of his or her life both on and off the field of athletic competition.

ABOUT THE AUTHORS

DEVIN DURRANT

Devin Durrant led Provo High School's basketball team to the 1978 3A Utah State Championship. He scored 38 of his team's 52 points in the final game. Devin made the All-State team and was named the 3A Most Valuable Player. He was also named to the McDonald's All-American team and played in various All-Star games around the country. In the 1978 Derby Festival Basketball Classic, Devin won the one-on-one competition in the morning and was named the MVP of the game later that same evening. He graduated from Provo High School with academic honors.

Devin went on to play for four years at Brigham Young University. He was a starter in every game during his four-year career and was part of WAC championship teams for three of his four college years. He also competed three times in the NCAA post-season tournament. He was a two-time selection to the All-Western Athletic Conference first team and was twice named as a GTE/CoSida Academic All-American. Devin took a break from basketball after his sophomore year to serve for two years as an LDS missionary in Spain. He returned from Spain for his remaining two years of college basketball.

During Devin's senior year (1983-84) he became the leading single-season scorer in BYU history with 866 points. He finished the year as the third-leading scorer in the NCAA. During that same year he was named District 7 Player of the Year, *Associated Press* All-American, Basketball Writers Association All-American, National Association of Basketball Coaches All-American, *Sporting News* All-American, UPI All-American, and John Wooden All-American.

Devin graduated in the spring of 1984 from Brigham Young University in American Studies. After his graduation he was named as a recipient of an NCAA postgraduate scholarship. Later that summer, Devin was chosen by the Indiana Pacers as the 25th pick in the NBA draft. He played a season with the Pacers and part of a second season with the Phoenix Suns.

In a *Deseret News* poll in the year 2000, Devin was voted one of the top 10 college basketball players in Utah of the 20th century. In that same year, *Sports Illustrated* magazine named him one of the 50 most influential sports figures in Utah.

After Devin graduated from college he conducted his own basketball camp for nine years. Most recently, he worked for three years as an assistant basketball coach for the Timpanogos High School girl's team.

During and after his athletic career, Devin has been a speaker for numerous youth groups. He has also been actively involved as a volunteer, serving and counseling hundreds of young adults over the past twenty years.

Devin was born in Brigham City, Utah and raised in Utah and Kentucky. He and his wife Julie are the parents of six children. Devin owns various real estate companies.

GEORGE DURRANT

George Durrant is the author of more than 20 books, including the bestsellers *Love at Home—Starring Father* and *Don't Forget the Star*. He taught religion at Brigham Young University and worked in many capacities for the LDS Church Education System. He also served as director of Priesthood Genealogy for the LDS Church.

His education includes a B.S. degree in Art from BYU, a Master's degree in Educational Administration from BYU and an EdD degree in Educational Administration from BYU.

George was born and raised in American Fork, Utah and is married to the former Marilyn Burnham. He is the father of eight children and grandfather of 32 and counting.

FOOTNOTES

Preface
1   Brian Kilmeade, *The Games Do Count*, Regan Books, p. 56.

Part 1 – The Dream
1   Paul O'Neill with Burton Rocks, *Me and My Dad*, Perennial, p. 23.

Part 2 – Be Your Own Coach
1   Lance Armstrong with Sally Jenkins, *Every Second Counts*, Broadway Books, p. 147.
2   Bill Bradley, *Values of the Game*, Broadway Books, p. 2.
3   Susan Valentine, *Carly Patterson*, Razorbill, p. 145.
4   Lance Armstrong with Sally Jenkins, *Every Second Counts*, Broadway Books, pp. 38-39.
5   Bill Bradley, *Values of the Game*, Broadway Books, p. 56.
6   Larry Bird with Bob Ryan, *Drive: The Story of My Life*, Bantam Books, p. 153.
7   Bill Bradley, *Values of the Game*, Broadway Books, p. 55.
8   Pat Riley, *The Winner Within*, Berkley Books, p. 149.
9   Rick Pitino with Bill Reynolds, *Success Is A Choice*, Broadway Books, p. 193.
10 Pat Williams with Michael Weinreb, *How To Be Like Mike*, Health Communications, p. 30.
11 Rick Pitino with Bill Reynolds, *Success Is A Choice*, Broadway Books, pp. 58-59.
12 Charles Barkley with Michael Wilbon, *I May Be Wrong, But I Doubt It*, Random House, p. 226.
13 John McEnroe with James Kaplan, *You Cannot Be Serious*, Berkley, p. 118.

Part 3 – Be Coachable
1   Larry Platt, *Only The Strong Survive*, Regan Books, pp. 34-35.
2   Larry Bird with Bob Ryan, *Drive: The Story of My Life*, Bantam Books, p. 4 and p. 27.
3   John Feinstein, *Season On The Brink*, Simon and Schuster, p. 86.
4   Bill Bradley, *Values of the Game*, Broadway Books, pp. 24-25.

5   Charles Barkley with Michael Wilbon, *I May Be Wrong, But I Doubt It*, Random House, p. 201.

6   Larry Platt, *Only The Strong Survive*, Regan Books, p. 192.

7   John Wooden with Steve Jamison, *A Lifetime of Observations and Reflections On and Off the Court*, Contemporary Books, pp. 152-153.

8   Pat Summitt with Sally Jenkins, *Reach for the Summit*, Broadway Books, p. 39.

Part 4 - Work, Work, Work

1   Lance Armstrong with Sally Jenkins, *Every Second Counts*, Broadway Books, p. 155.

2   Pat Conroy, *My Losing Season*, Doubleday, p. 211.

3   Dale Murphy with Brad Rock and Lee Warnick, *MURPH*, Bookcraft, pp. 28-29.

4   L. Jon Wertheim, *Venus Envy*, Perennial, pp. 15-16.

5   Joe Layden, *Kobe*, Harper, pp. 129-130.

6   Lance Armstrong with Sally Jenkins, *Every Second Counts*, Broadway Books, p. 120.

7   Lance Armstrong with Sally Jenkins, *Every Second Counts*, Broadway Books, p. 160.

8   Rick Pitino with Bill Reynolds, *Success Is A Choice*, Broadway Books, p. 40.

9   Rick Pitino with Bill Reynolds, *Success Is A Choice*, Broadway Books, pp. 62-63.

Part 5 – Rodeo Tough

1   David Halberstam, *Playing For Keeps*, Broadway Books, pp. 20-21.

2   Pat Williams with Michael Weinreb, *How To Be Like Mike*, Health Communications, p. 173.

3   Dean Smith with John Kilgo and Sally Jenkins, *A Coach's Life*, Random House, pp. 158-159.

4   Pat Summitt with Sally Jenkins, *Reach for the Summit*, Broadway Books, p. 217.

5   David Halberstam, *Playing For Keeps*, Broadway Books, p. 99.

6   Larry Bird with Jackie MacMullan, *Bird Watching*, Warner Books, p. 20.

7   Phil Jackson and Hugh Delehanty, *Sacred Hoops*, Hyperion, p. 175.

Part 6 – Dare Mighty Things

1   Charles Barkley with Michael Wilbon, *I May Be Wrong, But I Doubt It*, Random House, p. 24.
2   John McEnroe with James Kaplan, *You Cannot Be Serious*, Berkley, p. 131.
3   David Halberstam, *Playing For Keeps*, Broadway Books, p. 21.
4   John Wooden with Jack Tobin, *They Call Me Coach*, Contemporary Books, p. 132.
5   Pat Williams with Michael Weinreb, *How To Be Like Mike*, Health Communications, p. 97.
6   Rick Pitino with Bill Reynolds, *Success Is A Choice*, Broadway Books, pp. 247-248.
7   Matt Christopher, *On the Field with Mia Hamm*, Little, Brown and Company, pp. 25-27.

Part 7 – Love the Game

1   Larry Bird with Bob Ryan, *Drive: The Story of My Life*, Bantam Books, pp. 5-6 and pp. 46-47.
2   Larry Bird with Bob Ryan, *Drive: The Story of My Life*, Bantam Books, pp. 46-47.
3   David Beckham, *Beckham: Both Feet on the Ground*, Harper Collins, p. 17.
4   David Beckham, *Beckham: Both Feet on the Ground*, Harper Collins, pp. 57-58.
5   Larry Bird with Bob Ryan, *Drive: The Story of My Life*, Bantam Books, p. 21.

Part 9 – Gifts from God

1   Pat Williams with Michael Weinreb, *How To Be Like Mike*, Health Communications, p. xxiv.
2   Paul O'Neill with Burton Rocks, *Me and My Dad*, Perennial, p. 70.
3   Pat Riley, *The Winner Within*, Berkley Books, pp. 132-133.
4   Charles Barkley with Michael Wilbon, *I May Be Wrong, But I Doubt It*, Random House, p. 33 and p. 36.